Dedicated to the Memory of

Doc Easter
1889-1967

and

Johnny Easter
1915-2009

Cocktails
of the
South Pacific
and Beyond

Advanced Mixology

by

Greg Easter

International Cuisine Press

2009

First Edition
(corrrected)

Table of Contents

Foreword

"A bartender serves people. A mixologist serves liquor."

This is not a cocktail book! At least not in the sense you would expect these days. Anyone looking for an encyclopedia of bar recipes can find a dozen or more choices at any corner bookstore. If that's too much trouble, then you can simply point and click your way to tens of thousands of named drink recipes online. So why would *anyone* write yet another book on such an exhausted topic? Because this is *not* an encyclopedia of cocktail recipes. This book is about aspects that have not been published before, or at least not for decades. Perhaps it is more of a philosophy. That philosophy begins with a reminder that the art of mixology does not rest in pouring some measured ingredients out of a shaker and then waiting for applause. Absolutely anyone can do that. True artistry lies in finding your own voice, and the foundation for that is in understanding how ingredients work with—or against—each other, and in rethinking some of the faulty old ideas about mixing. This book is a blend of new ideas and old secrets. Some of these ideas have been in my family for a century now. Some ideas are the result of my own discoveries while traveling around the world. I am confident that even the most seasoned professional will discover something new and worthwhile within these pages.

For the record, I have intentionally avoided reprinting well known recipes here as much as possible. While there are a few classic drinks covered (*e.g.* the Margarita, Scorpion, Zombie), the approach presented here is such a radical departure from the traditional approach that these versions could easily be given new names and claimed as original. My departed friend, Victor *Trader Vic* Bergeron once wrote, "You know, bartending is a lot of hokum. You leave out one ingredient, or put in another and give the thing a different name, and you've got a new drink." Indeed, Vic's own books are chock full of examples of this; many recipes that are nearly identical to one another. This is not a criticism of him, though. He found his own voice, and expressed his philosophy in every recipe that he created. The personal preferences of a mixologist can not be separated from the types of drinks that he or she creates. Trader Vic was a devoted enthusiast of rum in its pure form. He preferred drinks that would not mask the natural flavors of the rum itself. It is a bit ironic that his recipes do not actually specify the fine rums that he used, but there is a reason for that.

Let's consider his most famous drink, the classic *Mai Tai*. In 1944 when Trader Vic invented this drink, he was using 17-year old J. Wray & Nephew rum. His cost for that was low enough that he could still turn a profit at about a dollar a cocktail. Today that same rum costs thousands of dollars a bottle, if you can even find it—and you probably can't. But cheer up! If you want an original Mai Tai made with the very same original ingredients as he poured in 1944, it is still served at the Merchant Hotel in Belfast, Ireland. The price is $1,500 per drink. Bottoms up!

The old top-shelf rums that were favored by the likes of Don the Beachcomber and Trader Vic in their glory days are virtually all extinct. Examples included Myers's "Mona", aged 30 years, and Lemon Hart "Rare Old", aged 28 years. These rums have not been produced for a very long time. When the occasional bottle does show up at auction, the gavel goes down at an extraordinary price far beyond the means of mere mortal men.

How did this happen? In the 1940's there was relatively little demand for rum, and the value of the dollar on the world market was very high. If you were mixing cocktails with liquor that was of such quality, you can easily understand the philosophy of being careful not to cover up the flavor of such a fine rum with loads of fruit juice and sugar. Today the best rum that you are likely to be using for cocktails is quite inferior to what was being poured freely half a century ago. The origins of this problem can be seen all the way back in the 1950's, as Trader Vic himself had to keep lowering his rum standards successively on repeated occasions as the demand for fine rums increased, causing supplies to become unreliable and prices to climb. This has been documented in numerous other books and sources, including Trader Vic's own website.

What this comes down to is that the days of affordable, transcendently fine rum are gone forever. Consequently, the mantra of the 1950's to use a minimalist approach of only lightly flavoring rum cocktails so as not to mask the exquisite perfume and structure already present in the liquor, must be erased from the mind of today's mixologist. These days you *will* be working with only a medium quality of rum compared to what was available decades ago, and so the idea of carefully respecting the ambrosia-like flavor is ridiculous, unless you have the budget of a drunken billionaire.

Rather than trying to deny the lesser quality of commercial rums today, we must accept this fact of life and revive some of the even older prohibition-era techniques to obtain outstanding results with good quality—but not the absolute finest—spirits. As I said at the start, this is *not* a book with a thousand recipes that have already been published. This is a method and a style that is the culmination of three generations of mixologists in my family, dating back to the late 19th century, and perfected with thousands of experiments—and dozens of livers! Just as some readers will adore these new ideas, undoubtedly there will be others who would object to sanctioning a break with the traditions. Only there is no real break here. Some of the ideas here have been in practice in the finest establishments for decades. Others have been mixed into your favorite cocktail without you even being aware of it, in the form of what went into the bottled mix being used, or even the liquor itself in some instances. The main difference here is that I am showing you how to take control of those ingredients yourself directly, and use them to create more sophisticated flavors. Whether that means a powerfully intense flavor that blows you away, or a faint underlying infusion that adds a sense of genuine quality to a classic drink on a subliminal level, will be up to you.

If you like simple recipes that you can throw together in less than a minute, then you will find most of the concepts and recipes here painfully tedious. On the other hand, if you are weary of the wimpy sugar water that passes for a cocktail these days, and you are tired of your only two options coming down to adding still *more* sugar, or to adding still *more* alcohol, then this book will give you some new avenues to explore.

Mixology is an art as much as it is a science. No two individuals will agree about everything, but I can confidently state that there are a few novel ideas here that you will *not* find in *any* other cocktail book ever published. Unlike a typical cocktail recipe book, this is a book that you should really try to read from front to back. It has been organized and written with the expectation that the reader is already familiar with the basics.

I want to encourage every mixologist to break free of outdated philosophies and antiquated conventions, not the least of which is this absurd notion of measuring ingredients in ponies and jiggers. This is the 21st century, for crying out loud! Milliliters have been used throughout this book. Precision in the control of proportions is essential to the art of flavor. You can not create a fine oil painting on a canvas using house paint and a roller. You need quality ingredients and sufficiently small units of measurement to control the balance of those flavors.

"Sometimes Wisdom Tells Us Lies"

Just as the concept of cocktail minimalism is no longer realistic—as just explained above—there is a second corollary to this truth. The common wisdom of the past was that *simplicity* produces the best results. That is, fewer ingredients somehow makes for a better drink. This was blindly accepted for decades, despite obvious evidence to the contrary right in front of everyone. Namely a beverage served at virtually every single bar in the entire world: Coke. This semi-secret formula contains a bewildering array of unlikely ingredients, which is why it tastes unlike anything else. This realization is a cornerstone on which some of the finest restaurants and bars on the planet have based their signature liquid creations. As an example of this trend, consider the menu at *Mango Tree*, an outstanding cutting edge bar with locations in London, Bangkok and Dubai. A typical offering from their menu is the *Green Penka* cocktail, with a list of nine ingredients, including ultra premium vodka, apple schnapps, melon liqueur, apple juice, Mascarade liqueur, various muddled fresh fruits, etc.

The cutting edge of mixology today lies in the realization that it is acceptable to layer and blend flavors, and that concealing some of the flavor of the liquor itself is not always a bad thing. In fact, most consumers would prefer to have the alcohol portion of the cocktail play a background role. Note that this is in sharp contrast to consumer preferences a few decades ago, when the most frequent complaint would be that you "can't even taste the alcohol." Thus, the premise of cocktail books from that era are often at odds with today's market.

 ❦

Chapter 1

Our History in the Liquor Trade

My grandfather began in 1908—More than a century ago.

What separates the great bartenders from the hacks is the understanding that mixology is a sophisticated art with a lot in common with magic. It is not real magic, of course. It is a matter of taking steps ahead of time that the customer is unaware of. Just as a magician prepares stage illusions, and the audience is left baffled because they didn't see him stuffing those rabbits into his pockets a moment before he came on stage, the same approach can be used in mixology, as I am about to describe.

First let me address a natural question that any reader might ponder. Why should I be the one to write such a book? Because of both my personal experience spanning nearly half a century, and from my own family who began producing and bottling spirits in 1908. It was not until I was well into my forties and began avidly collecting vintage cocktail books as a hobby that I began to fully appreciate just how remarkable my own life has been in regard to the liquor trade.

My grandfather, "Doc", began working at a Kansas City

bourbon distillery in 1908. When prohibition was passed in 1919, he moved on to become a significant player in the bootlegging industry in the area.

There were two historical epochs in the world of alcoholic beverages during the 20th century. Prohibition was the first of these, and this has been expounded upon by many authors in other books already. In short, the horrible tasting bathtub gin that was available during prohibition could only be consumed with the aid of a lot of sugar and flavorings. Most straight liquor of that period was said to be so foul that not even the most determined hobo could swallow a full glass without promptly vomiting it back up. If you can't hold it down, you can't get drunk. An interesting thing is that deliberately getting drunk was frequently the goal at that time. The phrase *drink responsibly* was not in their vocabulary. The paradox was that being able to drink a lot without actually becoming drunk was one of the most venerable traits of manliness.

The desire to *not* get plastered generated yet another rebirth of the cocktail. One looks a bit silly nursing a shotglass of vodka for twenty minutes. Mix that same ounce of liquor into a cocktail, and the impression by others at your table has been elevated to that of civilized restraint. Polite society tends to judge someone who orders their third glass in a row of straight bourbon as an alcoholic. Yet the same person can sit behind a gigantic drink containing twice as much liquor with impunity, as long as that said drink is sufficiently decorated with kabobs of tropical fruit and paper umbrellas. If you are on a date, ordering an entire bottle of scotch is probably going to be interpreted as a serious red flag. Yet several decades ago this was perfectly acceptable etiquette. In fact, you might even impress your date with your machismo by finishing off the bottle over a couple of cigars, just the way her dear old Dad would have. Still more recently you probably couldn't even find a bar that would serve you an entire bottle of hard liquor unless there were at least ten people at your table. Times have changed and this is one of the reasons why cocktails are back...again.

Virtually every cocktail book for several decades now has concentrated on simplifying recipes for the amateur. The net result has been the near total loss the science and art of mixology itself. If you doubt this, then skip ahead here to the Appendix (page 243) for a look at what was involved in making drinks in 1928. I have chosen a middle ground in this book with recipes that are far more involved than usually seen today, but still not requiring a degree in chemical engineering.

The other period of historical significance that is less often emphasized in cocktail lore, was World War II. By the 1930's, liquor quality was excellent and there was no social taboo against drinking a glass of straight hard liquor. Mixology and bartending were almost two different realms, as strange as that seems now. Popular cocktails were quite simple affairs, such as the *Sidecar* and the *Manhattan*. Exotic cocktails were for eccentric aristocrats. Only women would order very sweet drinks. Then suddenly the biggest war in all of modern history broke out. Young men who had been drinking soda pop and malt shop sundaes, suddenly found themselves transported onto battlefields under terrifying conditions. Almost everyone took to drinking and smoking as a way to help cope with the pressure of their comrades being maimed and killed all around them. The trouble was that drinking hard liquor straight is not something one can just rush into, no matter how dire the circumstances. Especially when the quality of liquor you were getting during war time tasted a lot like the same fuel your jeep was running on. The most basic lesson of prohibition was revived again: Sugar helps make inferior liquor go down easier. For those in the South Pacific theater, sweet tropical fruit was readily available. The idea of mixing it with liquor was obvious, but elevating those concoctions into the malt shop equivalent of a truly delicious beverage was a valuable commodity that could win you many friends. It could also be exploited for profit. This happened to be an art that my father already had years of practice with long before Pearl Harbor. A makeshift bar could be cobbled together in a few hours with spare lumber on the ship, especially in areas where abandoned buildings were available for the taking. With shiploads of sailors and marines who were about to leave for battle, or were just returning from hell on earth, it was no surprise that business was spectacular.

You may be wondering how my father happened to have experience in mixology. Like Don the Beachcomber, my father's experience also began during prohibition in the 1920's. The entire family had been involved in both the manufacture and transportation of bootleg liquor. One of his uncles was in charge of building cars that no police cruiser could catch. Their "wagon" could travel at up to 70 miles an hour over dirt roads. In the days before police radio, a high speed vehicle made you practically invulnerable. Uncle Roy's contribution was a homemade automotive supercharger. Although that technology already existed for race cars in Germany and France, he made one that would work on stock production line American cars. They later applied the name "supercharged" to a method of citrus fruit preparation for cocktails that is used frequently in this book.

A serious dispute between two crime syndicates in Kansas City had resulted in a contract being put out for Doc, and the entire family packed up and left for California in the middle of the night while they still could. Driving a nondescript plain black Model-T Ford across half of the United States when there were no highways, the trip took 19 days. Most of the way you couldn't go much more than a few miles an hour over rocks and across fields. This was 1932, when one could disappear without a trace just by moving to another state.

My father in front of his first establishment on an island of the Philippines.

They initially arrived in Long Beach, but the economy there was so bad that they soon moved a second time to Oakland.

Prohibition was repealed shortly after they arrived, and the bottom fell out of the bootleg liquor industry. Legal liquor was better quality and less expensive. Bootleggers had to find a new line of work. For my grandfather, that meant finding a new way to charge a lot of money for the same liquor. He did.

After having completed a mail order course in chiropractic medicine, my grandfather opened his own doctor's office and became known as "Doc" to friends and family alike. There he bottled and prescribed gin-based alcoholic libations to his patients as patent medicines. In those days the government rarely got involved in medical treatments, and a "doctor was a doctor" in the eyes of the law—even a mail order chiropractor. Doc became a such popular local character that even years after he died I would walk into that neighborhood and elderly strangers would enthusiastically shake my hand on the street, remembering me as his grandson. You see, in the years that followed the repeal of prohibition, many Americans still considered drinking as something sinful. But if you called a cocktail "medicine" and a "doctor" had ordered you to drink it, then it was a guilt-free pleasure. Doc flavored his volatile medications with sugary fruit syrups, using the same recipes that he had been selling in Kansas City as cocktails. His "medicines" were to be kept cold in the refrigerator and sipped directly from the bottle with a straw, while relaxing. Those were Doc's exact orders!

What makes this history especially interesting is that his doctor's office happened to be located on the 6400 block of

San Pablo Avenue in Oakland, just a couple of hundred feet from Trader Vic's original 1934 establishment. They all knew each other, and they spent time at his restaurant with "Uncle Vic" (as I was encouraged to call him as a child at the time).

The matchbook cover shown above is actually from a few years later, after Victor had expanded to a second location in Hawaii (T.H. stood for Territory Hawaii, before it became a state). The tremendous success of Trader Vic's led to many other copycat Polynesian theme bars and restaurants in the same neighborhood. One such place was Zombie Village, which shamelessly opened up right across the street from Vic's.

While Doc was having good success marketing his "medicinal" liquors out of his chiropractic office, my father, Johnny, had built a career in the U.S. Merchant Marine just before the second World War broke out. The ships that he worked on travelled between the West Coast of the United States and the Orient (as it was called in those days). Contrary to popular belief, this was actually the most dangerous branch of the service to be in during war time. One in twenty-six members of the entire U.S. Merchant Marine died during the course of the war. Over half received serious injuries. Consider that these ships operated in hostile waters, generally unarmed and unescorted, and often carried flammable and explosive materials that made the ship a floating bomb. Aviation fuel was the worst cargo. It was so volatile that the crew had to wear special shoes that did not have nails in the soles, so as not to ignite the fumes on the deck as they walked. To this day there are more than thirty ships that remain unaccounted for. They are presumed sunk with all hands, which may have been from enemy attack, or simply an accident onboard in which no one survived. My father survived the sinking of two ships during this period. One that was hit by a torpedo, and the other due to a collision with another ship in heavy fog.

Although he spent time on several merchant vessels over the years, most of the cocktail-related adventures that are mentioned in this book happened while he was the Second Mate (navigator)

The SS Linfield Victory

on the Linfield Victory. During the war they delivered equipment and supplies to troops, as well as having had the unpleasant task of filling body bags with the less fortunate souls from battlefields, to bring back home for a proper burial.

Often the carnage was so great that it was impossible to tell what body part belonged with which torso, and unbeknownst to their families, body bags were frequently filled by weight and volume with remains. As if this wasn't gruesome enough, in New Guinea they would arrive to collect corpses and find that the majority had no heads. The natives would come in the night and collect them to make shrunken heads. They believed that these heads would bring them strength and vitality when hung outside of their homes. It was better if you had killed the person yourself, but still a head is a head, and suddenly their jungle was filled with free heads for the taking. Where once a powerful tribal chief might have had three or four heads hanging outside of his shack, now they would see row after row of heads in front of almost every house. It was obvious that these were not the result of a war with other natives, because the features were clearly Caucasian and Japanese. To make matters worse, the natives also liked to collect the dogtags of their trophies, making the task of figuring out who's body parts were laying in the jungle even more difficult. This problem escalated to new heights after the natives learned that the dogtags were somehow prized items to these white men, who would reward them richly for a basket full of these shiny do-dads. An odd kind of alliance was formed, as the natives were masters at combing the jungles for these dogtags, and since they had no practical use for them, they were very happy to trade them in for sugar, salt, spices, liquor, or whatever else was available. What is truly ironic is if not for the diligent work of these cannibals, there would have been hundreds more MIA's. Unfortunately, the downside was that the person named on the body bag often had nothing to do with the contents. There was nothing that anyone could do about that.

The skill of these headhunters at hiding in the jungles was astonishing. Accompanied by armed U.S. Marines who were experts at jungle warfare, crewmembers of the Merchant Marine vessels would go through the bush looking for corpses. The marines could spot a Japanese ambush hiding in trees from 400 yards away, but they would never see any of the native headhunters. Yet when they shot an enemy out of a tree, by the time they got to the body on the ground, sometimes it was already decapitated! The natives were everywhere, and nowhere. They knew the terrain better than anyone else could, of course. Hunting people in those jungles had been their way of life for generations. Their survival had depended on it long before the United States even existed.

Trader Vic's original location had several shrunken heads on display in a glass case as you entered the restaurant. Now you know where they came from.

Within a few years my father had risen to the position of navigator. This was at a time when ships would typically take a month to cross the Pacific Ocean. When they arrived at their destination, the loading and unloading of cargo would take several days. Sometimes more than a week. There were no standard size containers in those days. Everything was loaded into the holds by physically carrying it and stacking it. Wooden crates were constructed to secure cargo, and it was held in place with ropes and chains. Everything was by hand, including balancing the load. You couldn't have a ship loaded so that all the weight was at one end, or when it got into a storm, the ship would be likely to sink. This manual loading and arranging of cargo provided opportunities for looting, as you can well imagine. Particularly vulnerable were cases of liquor, which were like liquid gold. It was estimated that for every twenty cases of liquor shipped to officers and generals, only one would actually arrive to the intended recipient.

On one of the trips he made, a staff car for General Douglas MacArthur was being shipped to him. Whoever was sending it had filled the front seat, the back seat, and the trunk with cases of fine liquors. The car came with two military police officers who would accompany the shipment to personally ensure that it actually arrived safely. As the crate containing the limousine was lowered down into the hold, my father made sure that he was the one arranging how the cargo was being stacked at the time. This was normally the work of lower ranking sailors, but as Second Mate he had the authority to relieve anyone and take over for them. From the point of view of the security guards, it seemed that the Captain was helping to take additional precautions that the shipment would be tied down securely. After the car was in place, countless other crates of assorted goods continued to fill in the cargo hold, until it was stacked up to the top, as was normally done. With the car buried beneath hundreds of crates, the security guards were no longer concerned about anything happening to their crate during the voyage. What they had not realized was that my father had carefully mapped out exactly where the crate was located within that cargo hold. Having weeks to work on it as they made their way across the Pacific Ocean, he opened up one of the emergency doors at the bottom of the ship and gradually tunneled his way through every crate between that doorway and the box containing the car. With the help of a couple of other crew members, they got inside and disassembled the car from the bottom to gain access inside of the passenger compartment and the trunk, and unloaded every single crate of liquor, carrying it out one box at a time through the tunnel they had created. Then they reassembled the car, sealed up the crate, and put every other crate that had been moved back in place in the same order that it had been removed from, so it all fit perfectly. When the ship finally reached its berth and the cargo was unloaded, the military police were horrified and astonished that there was no longer a single box inside the car! They searched the entire ship, but no one seemed to know anything about it (naturally). The liquor had been transferred into the anchor room behind a false steel wall that had been welded in place and painted over so that it looked like any other part of the ship. They could have searched the ship for the rest of their lives and never found it. They agreed to help the security guards out by signing a statement that there never had been any boxes inside the car when they picked it up. As soon as they reached the next port, the false wall in the anchor room was cut open and the booty was divided up. The other sailors wanted the whiskey, which worked out perfectly because my father was mostly interested in the cases of French cognac and flavored liqueurs that were otherwise nearly impossible to obtain. He estimated that he made over $10,000 from that caper, which in 1940's money was a small fortune.

The duties of the navigator were less demanding than that of the other deck officers — and more important, while in port, he generally had time off. In those days they would tie up to a dock for a week, or even longer. During that time he was able to explore whatever country they happened to be in. He could have advanced his career on up to captain, but that would have meant that he had to stay onboard the ship when they were in port. He was making much more money than the captain with his side business enterprises that he ran while he was ashore, and he had more free time than anyone else on the ship to follow his own pursuits. Although he dabbled in the import-export business, his main business was operating these fly-by-night bars for soldiers.

When my father was in port in California, he would visit his father, Doc, who lived upstairs from his chiropractic office at that time. They would often go to Trader Vic's a few doors down. My father would regale Vic with his most recent exploits, and at least some of those stories were woven into the fabric of Vic's colorful tales of his "own adventures" that he would spin for customers. All in good fun, of course.

Having grown up in a family that produced liquor, and then compounded by his exposure to Trader Vic, it was a natural curiosity for my father to learn more about how natives in Polynesia made their alcoholic beverages. Many of these rather crude and sharp tasting liquors were already being mixed with tropical fruit juices by the natives themselves to make more palatable drinks, in much the same fashion as bathtub gin had been during prohibition.

My father's mother (my grandmother) had died of cancer long before that time, and my grandfather remarried a woman who worked in the cosmetics department of the largest drug store in San Francisco. Through her employment at the drug store, she had connections for obtaining liquor, which was often scarce during World War II. She was able to obtain cases of fine liquors, which my father would pick up and take to soldiers in the Pacific. Initially he sold bottles of liquor just as they were, but then realized that profits would be much greater if he mixed them into cocktails instead. Especially when he was trying to sell gin or rum, which was not nearly as popular with soldiers as whiskey.

His "watering holes" were usually little more than abandoned shacks, and they moved location frequently as the war progressed and troops were stationed in different areas. This was never a serious business, but more something he would do for a few weeks at a time before running out of liquor, and getting back on the ship the next time it arrived back in port. At one point he tried to build a more permanent establishment in Legaspi, including getting a generator for

Legaspi Location

the building, and even finding local materials and building a bar out of teakwood. This was the longest running makeshift bar he ran, which he managed to keep going for several months continuously by incorporating native liquors to stretch out his supply of gin and medical alcohol (essentially high-proof vodka) that he had brought in. He closed the place down for a month to make a trip to get more liquor and supplies, and contemplated settling down there; to make a new life on land, and get away from the dangers of the war. When he returned a month later, someone had used a hand grenade to blast a hole in the back wall so that they could loot the place and steal the teakwood bar that my father had installed. The grenade had wiped out one wall of the building, leaving it in serious danger of collapsing at any moment. It also managed to destroy half the tables and chairs, as well as do serious damage to th electrical generator that was situated near the back door. The amount of work it would have taken to rebuild it was more than it took to find another location. That was the nature of the business in those days.

There were some occasions in which Johnny found himself stranded with nothing else to do all day, and so he worked at inventing drinks while relaxing. He was on a ship that was sunk by the Japanese, and after several days on a lifeboat, he had the remarkable good fortune of making it to shores of Rarotonga. It took two months before he could find someone with a radio to call to be picked up. Few white people had spent any significant time on the island at that point in history, and he became quite a local celebrity among the native Tongans, including Queen Salote. This was a long before her historic tour of England. He introduced Salote to a number of libations, including one included here that is named for her, and it has never before been published anywhere. Such tales were a delight to Trader Vic, of course.

Both my father and Victor Bergeron influenced each other in some ways, but I think that mostly they were a product of their time. They were not the only ones to capitalize on the public's interest in Polynesia. By the early 1940's, there were at least eight different Tropical theme clubs within a few blocks of each other in Oakland. At their peak, there were live orchestras. There was pseudo-Polynesian food and cocktails with every kind of crazy name they could think up. The bulk of the customers initially were sailors from the nearby ports of Alameda and San Francisco. Thousands of sailors were returning from active duty, or just on shoreleave. They had money to burn, and so this

thriving industry of nightlife was created practically out of thin air overnight.

Rather than simply open yet another bar on the strip, which was both expensive and risky (given the competition that already existed), Johnny and his war buddy/business partner Al came up with a new way to exploit the nightclub and dining gold mine that Oakland had turned into. This became known as the "camera concession" business. They rented a room upstairs in the attic of a building across the street from the Tropical Club, owned by friend Rudi Blaettler, in the heart of this strip of nightclubs at the time. They turned this small space into a high-speed darkroom in which they could process film and print photographs.

The camera concession business consisted of a small army of beautiful—and scantily clad—girls carrying Speedgraphic cameras. Customers who were dining with friends would pay a dollar to have a souvenir photo of themselves and their dinner party taken in the tropical ambience of one of these Disneyesque South Seas nightclubs.

The film would then be rushed upstairs to the darkroom, where it was quickly developed and printed. It was turned out in record time for that era. The chemicals were heated up to accelerate the process, and prints were dried on drum rollers in order to meet the demand for a turnaround time of under 20 minutes—almost unbelievable in those days. This helped to insure that the guest would still be in the same booth by the time the photo was ready. If the recipient liked the picture, they could order additional copies and enlargements at a higher price. At the peak of this era, Johnny and Al had over twenty girls walking around to all of the clubs in the area. The streets were packed every single night with patrons, and the profits were astounding.

Then, as suddenly as it had began…it was over. The war had ended and sailors were heading back to their home towns. The entire area turned into a ghost town within a span of two months. As my father would say, you could fire a

12th & Franklin St. as it appears today.
Their darkroom had been on the second floor.

cannon down 12th Street and not have to worry about hitting anyone. Soon there were only a few places that had managed to stay in business after that. One of those was Trader Vic's.

All of these nightclubs offered exotic decor and an array of fictional tropical cocktails with intriguing names, but most of them failed to deliver on quality. Trader Vic had learned how to produce almost magical cocktails that could not be duplicated by amateurs. Although he published several books with recipes for drinks of the same names as those in his restaurants, there were differences between what was actually being served and the printed recipes. Anyone who had a drink at Trader Vic's bar, then went home to duplicate the same drink out of his book, could see that the homemade version was only a crude approximation in some cases. I do not know how much of this was intentional, and how much was at the request of his publisher. Like Don the Beachcomber, drinks in the restaurant were concocted from blends of rums and other ingredients that were just not available to the general public. Even if Victor or Don had wanted to share exact secret recipes, what kind of person would purchase a dozen different hard-to-find liquors and combine small quantities of each one, then flavor the mixture with other herbs and spices and let it sit for months before using it? To make the recipes accessible to the general public, they had to be simplified with generic ingredients. No publisher would market a book that had the reader spending hundreds of dollars and several hours of time to produce a single cocktail. That kind of labor is only practical when you have a commercial establishment going, and you can prepare large batches that you will make a profit on. You might argue that such an effort would also be made by those with a genuine love for mixology, but publishers want mass market appeal for their books. They can not survive by publishing books that would sell only a few copies worldwide. Ironically, that was the same problem encountered when writing the book you are now holding in your hands. My goal here was not to create a detailed encyclopedia of every drink I have ever encountered, but rather to advocate a better philosophy in keeping with the ingredients are available these days, exemplified by some techniques that have been largely forgotten.

The new garde of mixologists concentrate on using fresh ingredients. This directly followed from the relatively recent trend in restaurants to provide food with "fresh and local ingredients." I put this in quotes because it has became a phrase that is so often repeated as to be almost silly. The importance of *fresh and local ingredients* is now the holy mantra of virtually every prestigious chef around the world. Credit for this is generally given to Alice Waters in the 1970's at *Chez Panisse*. The concept became such a cornerstone of fine dining that it was only a matter of time before it spilled over onto the closely allied field of high end mixology. Now we see bars where they are infusing liquors with locally grown herbs and growing their own fruit to produce novel syrups. Ripeness and freshness are important.

Making your own syrups from fresh fruit was just part of normal everyday work for ritzy bars at the turn of the last century. Although one old shortcut was dissolving store-bought fruit preserves in hot water, then straining off the solids. This was not such a bad idea back in the day when jams were made with cane sugar and natural ingredients. Unfortunately these days inexpensive jams contain synthetic flavoring agents that will come through as an unpleasant aftertaste in a drink to a discerning palate. Still, this trick is worth keeping in the back of your mind if you ever find yourself in need of a particular flavor that is hard to come by as a syrup, but you can find a *quality* jam of the same fruit.

Consumer expectations slowly and steadily declined, and corporate profits became the dominant factor in what ingredients were used at commercial establishments. In more recent times, concerns about the health effects of strong drinks and legal issues pertaining to intoxication also played a significant role in this decline of cocktail culture.

Still, the biggest enemy of quality remains the profit margin. After all, when a bottle of Sweet and Sour mix is $2 a quart, and lemons are $1 each, almost any business-minded owner will choose the mix, as long as customers don't object too strenuously. There was no single specific year when the art of the cocktail officially died. Rather, it died the death of a thousand cuts, as consumers gradually accepted lower and lower standards. Mass marketed mixers gained popularity, and many distilleries learned that it made sense to produce liquor that was not aged as long, because more volume meant more profit and their cellars only had so much space. These days the majority of the drinking public has never even sampled a classic cocktail the way it was originally intended to taste. Very few bars would even prepare such a drink, and even fewer patrons would be willing to pay for it.

Even during the so-called revival periods of the cocktail—and there have been several over the last half century—the *old* art of mixology has never been resurrected. Some of the tricks that produce the most extraordinary drinks have been pushed aside as being too time consuming, too complicated, or simply requiring ingredients that are no longer available. To some extent the latter is an inescapable reality. On the other hand, there is no shortage of quality ingredients that may be employed to produce libations that are as refined as anything ever produced in the last century. I say this from my own personal experience in tasting, which now spans nearly half a century.

SOME PERSONAL HISTORY

One of my earliest childhood memories is my father and Victor Bergeron playing some kind of dice game at his bar. Vic was having the bartender serve me Shirley Temples while telling me some stories about the actress who was the namesake of my drink. I still remember him leading my father and me on a private tour of a back room in which he blended rums and spiked them with spoonfuls of exotic ingredients before the bottles were "put to bed" to let the mixtures steep. It was several decades later when I discovered that very few people had ever been allowed into that locked room.

I grew up in a suburb of the Bay Area near Trader Vic's original location. A couple of miles in the other direction was an unusual business with a related theme, Trader Jim's *Horns of the Hunter*. The logo was the head of a rhinoceros on a liquor barrel, surrounded by the name. The anchor store was "that liquor joint with the buggy on the roof", but the entire complex was owned by the same person, including a tropical theme bar and a banquet hall where he served game meats.

As a child, this all seemed perfectly typical. My father had explored the world, and so had his friends. That's what most every adult male I knew had done. They all had their stories about encounters with wild animals and even wilder natives.

At the Horns of the Hunter, you drove into the parking lot under the actual jaw bone of a whale. The liquor store's walls were decorated with trophy heads of different game animals. There was a stuffed polar bear in a glass case in one corner. Next to this liquor store was a taxidermist whose work in progress was exhibited in the window there. A bit further down was a special events "Hunting Lodge" with a tropical grass roof, where banquets were hosted by the owner. You had to have an invitation to attend these affairs, and pay an admission for the evening. The dinners featured game meats of animals killed by Trader Jim. What was really unusual is that he would show home movies and slides taken during the hunting expedition that was responsible for bringing down the very game that you were presently eating. Deer, elk and

moose were most frequently served, but also sometimes more exotic animals.

My father was invited to this group regularly and I was usually the only child who was allowed in. There was a lot of drinking—as you can well imagine considering that the host of the event was also the owner of the liquor store next door! I remember many high-octane punch bowls being consumed, and guests laughing in delight that I was holding my own with them drinking. Times were different, and the ability to hold one's liquor was an admirable trait at any age. Although technically the consumption of liquor by minors was against the law, there was an understanding back then that in private parties with a consenting parent along, it was just not something that would be prosecuted. Most children had tried beer and wine by the time they were ten years old, but even back in those permissive times I was exceptional for having full glasses of beer and wine with dinner occasionally. Because my parents had spent years among less restrictive cultures, they were especially lenient in that regard. As for the theory that it leads to teenage alcoholism, I should point out that when other teenagers were discovering the "joys" of getting wasted out of their minds, such behavior was of no interest to me because the effects of alcohol had never been a taboo temptation. Liquor was just another beverage, and moderation was as natural as breathing—and I don't hyperventilate for "fun" either. It is the same thing. Although, perhaps if I had spent my childhood in an atmosphere with very little oxygen, I might now find inhaling deeply to provide a cheap thrill.

THE 1980's

I finally left the Bay Area and moved to Hollywood, California, back in 1982. I spent the next 25 years there. One of my favorite restaurants became the Lobster Barrel, owned by Alan Hale, mostly remembered for his role as the Skipper in the television farce comedy, *Gilligan's Island*. But this was more than just another lobster and steak 

house on La Cienega. Back in the 1950's to 1960's this area was known as "Restaurant Row" and it was home to some of the finest restaurants on the entire West Coast. By the mid-1980's most of the great places were gone, though. The coming of the 1984 Summer Olympics in Los Angeles initiated a terrible transformation of the city. The sudden mass marketed corporate invasion that sought to capitalize on the coming Olympic crowds changed the landscape and the *feeling* of the city in what seemed like the blink of an eye.

Many of the old and familiar classic places were either torn down or revamped by their new corporate owners. The nostalgic days of Hollywood's Golden Age became lost in a maze of fast food franchises and mini malls. There were literally six McDonald's restaurants in the space of a few city blocks, not a single one of which had existed before 1983. Two of them closed down shortly after the Olympics were over, leaving boarded-up rotting shells behind that remained vacant for years. Historic landmarks were wiped out because the existing building did not conform to the standard floorplan required by the new franchise owner. It was not only the buildings and businesses that had been affected, but also the spirit of the city itself. These new corporate owners wanted everything cleaned up and sterilized. While the real damage had been done before the 1984 Olympics actually began, the total facelift that Hollywood received took more than a decade to complete. More than a billion dollars was spent on a few blocks of Hollywood Blvd. alone. It is probably impossible for someone who did not personally live through this period in the city to understand how this would have a negative impact. For those of you who lived in New York City, this was the Los Angeles version of what happened to Times Square.

The Lobster Barrel managed to hang on a little longer than most, owing somewhat to tourists that came in to meet one of the only Hollywood personalities who was actually available almost every single night. But it also survived longer from the revenue of loyal local patrons such as myself, who visited often for the high quality of food and drink provided at a time when second rate chain restaurants were swallowing up the city.

Alan Hale's use of the term *Waterfront Cocktails* was intended to conjure images of folding chairs on a sunny beach with attendants offering up trays of vibrantly colored intoxicants decorated with Lilliputian umbrellas. That illusion was the idea behind every Tiki Bar, of course. Alan Hale tried to avoid being branded as just another tacky Tiki bar, yet still remain more interesting than the typical Hollywood celebrity-owned steakhouse joint. There were some Tikis in the decor, in fact, but also quite a lot of memorabilia from the set of Gilligan's Island, such as the *S.S. Minnow's* life preserver hanging on the wall in the entrance.

Right next door to the Lobster Barrel was Xavier Cugat's Mexican-theme restaurant, *Casa Cugat*. Although he was a famous band leader for over twenty years, these days Cugat is remembered largely for his disovery of, and risque marriage to the Latin blonde bombshell, Charo. Her story about why she married him changed over the years, but never the less, she was 15 years old and he was 66 when they were married—and no one really seemed to mind all that much. I think that fact alone proves it was a pretty different world in

1966. Charo spent time at both Alan Hale's and her husband's restaurant to mingle with customers on occasion. I doubt anyone complained that she was not even 21 years old yet at the time she was hanging out at the bar. Again, it was a different world. At the height of its success, Casa Cugat had grown into a small chain with eight locations, but the one on La Cienega was the first. It finally went up in flames after a "suspicious fire" following a sharp decline in business after the 1984 Olympics.

Incidentally, I happened to see Charo in Hawaii many years later at the Hilton Hawaiian Village Resort, where the famous mixologist Harry Yee had gained international fame with his creation of the Blue Hawaii cocktail there. In a conversation at the bar, she said in her own inimitable harebrained sexpot way, "Cock and tail. I think whoever put these words together for something that gets you drunk, was a very smart business person, no?"

Although it should go without saying, *always* measure your ingredients carefully. The proportions in the recipes here are the result of dozens, and sometimes hundreds of experiments. If the recipe calls for a quarter teaspoon of something, it was measured using a calibrated measuring spoon, as are sold in gourmet kitchen stores. It was not merely estimated roughly. If you want to taste the exact same drink being described in the text, your accuracy in measuring is essential. I implore you to please purchase and use a set of these spoons for making the drinks in this book.

Throughout this book I have refused to adhere to the absurd and archaic pony and jigger system, rarely do I specify a "dash" of something. In case you ever wondered, a *dash* was actually defined as 1/6th of a teaspoon in some older texts. To say that this is an awkward measurement is an understatement. The only thing worse is a recipe that calls for, "the juice of half a lemon." As anyone who has ever squeezed fruit knows, different specimens produce different amounts of juice, depending on the ripeness, how long it was stored, what part of the world you are in, and even just how diligent you are in trying to squeeze out every last drop. No one really knows for sure what some of the older drinks were exactly like because of these crude and quaint measurements.

Fine drinks require precision in measuring, so do yourself a favor and purchase a small graduated container that can measure down to the nearest 5 milliliters for metric proportions. When a recipe here calls for 45ml of gin, for example, be assured that this was arrived at through countless experiments and side-by-side blind taste tests in which 40 and 50ml quantities were compared. For those of you who insist on trying to use ounces, a table of conversions is provided in the Appendix on page 237.

Many of the recipes in this book call for a long list of ingredients. This increases your chances of leaving something out, so make a habit of following the recipe line-by-line from top to bottom. Every ingredient is important.

Unlike some mixologists, I have not left anything out, or provided any misleading measurements. In fact, every recipe in here has been carefully checked and every recipe actually made and tasted from an identical copy of the book you now hold in your hands.

 හ Y ౭

Chapter 2

Technical Background

"Nothing is as Simple as It Seems"

There are several distinct layers of flavors which combine to produce the overall synthesis of a cocktail. These include the individual flavor profiles of the liquors chosen, the mixers and the extracts, and/or bitters. Yet many bartenders behave as though one bad flavor will somehow serve to cover up the next bad flavor when they are mixed together. They will not hesitate to use the cheapest booze (preferably with a happy animal on the label), and then add that to an artificially flavored and colored chemical solution of citric acid in place of fresh juice, containing high-fructose corn syrup in place of sugar—as if two cents worth of actual sugar would drive them into bankruptcy. Finally, they try to mask all of these crimes with dilution from cups of ice. But starting out with premium ingredients is only the first step to improving the final result.

Liquors, as we shall see in a section yet to come, may include flavoring agents that have been allowed to steep for days, or weeks in the bottle. Bitters are already complex, but when you make your own, you open up another new dimension of flavors. The more you can personalize the ingredients you are using, the more distinctive and impressive the resulting cocktail will be.

The term *mixer* properly refers to aromatic wines and/or fruit juice, particularly citrus juices. It goes without saying (or at least it should) that fresh juice is essential in the case of lemon, lime, and grapefruit juice. Although in the United States, you may actually be better off using a quality bottled orange juice most of the time, because most oranges there are watery and even sour tasting. Finding an orange that delivers sweet and concentrated flavor is difficult these days in the United States. A bottled juice like Tropicana, is often better than what you can squeeze out of the fresh fruit you can buy in a supermarket. This is not an endorsement of bottled juice in cocktails, but more a condemnation of the fruit that is grown to look pretty and have a long shelf life at the expense of its flavor. On a positive note, certain times of the year there are small miniature crates of mandarin oranges in American stores, that will produce an acceptable juice. The bottom line is to taste everything before you use it. If you have lived your entire life in America, you may not even realize what oranges and grapefruit are supposed to taste like, believe it or not.

I also make an exception with pineapple juice in the United States, for the exact *opposite* reason. The quality of Dole's large canned pineapple juice is as good as freshly processed. Just transfer it to a clean plastic bottle, because once it has been opened it begins to react with the metal can. Air with acidic pineapple juice and metal makes nasty tasting pineapple rust. Keep it in the refrigerator for up to a week.

It is best to wait until you are making drinks before squeezing the juice for them. The fruit's natural skin "packaging" keeps the juice fresh. Once it has been squeezed, it begins to gradually change. That's not to say that the juice needs to be squeezed as each drink is being made. If there is a party, or you are producing cocktails for a commercial restaurant or bar, you can certainly juice fruit several hours ahead of time and store the juice in a refrigerator without any real change in flavor. Just try to keep the storage time minimal. Juicing ahead of time also provides an opportunity to doctor your fruit juices with trace component flavors. While it is nearly impossible to add a microliter of orange oil to a single drink, it is simple to add a couple of drops of that oil to a liter of freshly squeezed juice. Many gourmet kitchen stores sell small bottles of orange, lime, and lemon oils. If you shop online, you can even find grapefruit and pineapple oils. Use only natural food-grade oils, and never the artificial flavor. These are intensely flavored, so a few drops per liter is all you will need to boost the taste. Keep the effect subtle, so that the final cocktail *whispers quality*. Too much and it will seem artificial.

SUPERCHARGING YOUR CITRUS

One easy way of altering the essential balance of a drink containing a citrus juice, is to include the skin (zest) of the fruit in some way. Any chef will tell you that the outermost layer of skin of citrus contains high concentrations of the essential oils that are similar to the flavor of the fruit's juice. Within my own family, this idea originated during the Great Depression of the 1930's, when everyone was looking for ways to stretch money. Shaving the skin of citrus with a wood rasp (since culinary microplane graters had not been invented yet) was a way of getting more flavor out of each piece of fruit. That flavor is distinctive, and it produces cocktails that taste inherently different from those made with only the juice.

These days that idea is usually restricted to a twist of lemon or orange peel floating on top, and not actually integrated into the drink itself. If you go back a few decades, it was not unusual to cut a small piece of the skin and toss it into the shaker with the other ingredients. I prefer a different method. First use a microplane grater to take off the zest of the citrus fruit of choice. Do *not* grate the white pith beneath the skin. A light touch over only the outer (pigmented) portion of the skin is *all* you want. This zest is put in a fine mesh sieve strainer, and the fruit is then cut and squeezed so that the juice pours over the zest, through the strainer, and into a measuring container.

Sometimes a spirit is also poured over the zest in the

strainer. Vodka is the neutral flavored choices here, because alcohol will extract more of the oils than water. Press the zest against the mesh of the strainer with the back of a spoon, or your finger, to express as much of the liquid as possible. Combine the juice and the alcohol extract, and you have produced a SUPERCHARGED citrus. In the recipes in this book, directions are stated explicitly, but you can use this technique with any recipe.

Still not potent enough? (…and are you really *sure* about that?!) Then pour the entire mixture back over the same zest a couple more times to further intensify it. Beware that this will produce such a concentrated flavor that this will easily overpower almost anything else in a cocktail. In fact, frequently a useful balance is obtained by mixing *some* of the SUPERCHARGED citrus with some of the same juice that was just squeezed fresh to create a batch of moderately enhanced juice. The exact method will depend on the cocktail being made, and personal preference, as always.

This technique has a rather startling effect on some drinks, but it is not *always* an improvement. It will depend on the nature of the cocktail. This method is referenced in some of the recipes in this book, where it makes an absolutely invaluable contribution to the flavor. You will need a little practice to be able to measure small amounts of citrus zest accurately, and the difference of only a quarter teaspoon will have a large impact on the final outcome.

Orange juice that is treated in this manner will be considerably more sour. An excellent way to soften that sour edge is with Monin's *Curaçao Triple Sec* syrup. The proportion to add will be determined by taste. Just be careful not to over-sweeten the batch, because more syrup can always be added to a drink when it is made. Once

there is an excess of sugar, the batch is limited to use in very sweet drinks.

The effect of the SUPERCHARGED technique on grapefruit warrants some special attention. First, because the effect is less pronounced than it is with other citrus juices. Most of the natural oils seem to dissolve better in alcohol than they do in grapefruit juice, so I generally suggest using only liquor from the cocktail you are preparing as the means of extracting flavor from grapefruit zest.

It should also be noted that most grapefruit available in grocery stores in the United States are generally poor for cocktails. I won't even go into the horrors of canned grapefruit juice. The grapefruit that is available in most of Europe and Asia lacks that metallic aftertaste and pungent bitterness than American grapefruit often has. When the grapefruit juice component is a small percentage of the drink, you can get away with fresh squeezed Ruby Grapefruit. Be warned that the SUPERCHARGED method sometimes intensifies the metallic aftertaste, so be especially watchful for this. Taste it first. When I lived in the US, I avoided recipes that called for very much grapefruit zest or juice, but if you grew up with it, you might be used to it. Since moving to Europe, I have found that SUPERCHARGED grapefruit is a delicious component that never has any metal taste to it. It will depend on where you live and your own tastes, as usual. I realize that this advice is useless, since you aren't going to move to another country just to enjoy better tasting grapefruit juice. Just keep it in mind that you may not be tasting the intended flavor if you are using American grapefruit. Let me summarize this by saying that grapefruit juice in the United States is problematic, and in some cases it is worsened further by the SUPERCHARGED process. If you reside in Europe or Asia, then you can probably disregard this cautionary note.

"The Best Way to Learn is to Experiment"

When you are making drinks in this book that call for citrus zest, you must experiment some to see how much is too much. An excess happens very easily, because this is a very potent ingredient. Make a test drink up, leaving out only the citrus component you wish to test. Divide the mix into two glasses and add straight citrus in one glass, and the SUPERCHARGED citrus of the same fruit in the other glass. Compare the taste. An excellent learning experience here is a *Margarita*. Because the lime plays such a fundamental role, boosting its citrus oil character makes for a pronounced difference in the final drink. If done correctly it adds something mysterious and powerful, which is exactly what you should be aiming for at the highest level of mixology. Too much and it becomes overpowering. The following cocktail is also illustrative of this technique…

King Louie

You might imagine this has something to do with French aristocracy, but it was actually named after a certain animated orangutan you may recall from childhood. This has the flavor of the jungle, but the sophistication of man's red fire.

30 ml.	Dark Rum, Bacardi *Black*
30 ml.	Light Rum, 10 Cane
3/4 teaspoon	Orange Zest - see directions below
15 ml.	Banana Liqueur, Bols
20 ml.	Orange juice, fresh
10 ml.	Lemon juice, fresh
10 ml.	Lime juice, fresh
15 ml.	Natural Brown Sugar Syrup (page 53)

Grate the zest onto a fine mesh sieve and gather it into a small pile in the center, as usual. Slowly pour over the two rums. Pinch and press the zest to expel as much of the rum as possible, then discard the zest. Add the rest of the ingredients and shake with ice. Either strain into a chilled martini glass, or serve on the rocks if a weaker drink is desired.

NATURAL BROWN SUGAR SYRUP

To produce this syrup, add equal amounts of demerara sugar (available in organic food stores) and water to a sauce pan. Heat while stirring until dissolved. Add about ten drops of pure vanilla extract per cup of solution. Pass the solution through a fine mesh sieve before bottling it. Store in the refrigerator.

Try mixing a little of this Natural Brown Sugar Syrup with a quality dark rum and a twist of lemon. If you have been used to bottled syrups made with high fructose corn syrup, this experiment will open your eyes to what you have been missing.

Va-va-va Voom

This cocktail's name was inspired by it being a favorite of one of the camera girls. She was part Russian, so a vodka based drink seemed fitting. She was known locally as "Treasure Chest Betty" because she had an actual $50,000 insurance policy from Lloyds of London on her breasts. Having seen a few photos of her from the time, I think it is safe to say that she must have been at least as intoxicating as this cocktail. Remember that there were no silicone implants in the 1940's. This is a scarce example of a drink from this era that employed vodka. While vodka itself was not mass marketed to Americans until about a decade later, it did exist if you searched around. There were also, "neutral grain spirits" sold for commercial and medicinal applications in larger drug stores. This 95% alcohol could be diluted with water to obtain a kind of industrial grade vodka. These days you will not find neutral grain spirits for sale in drug stores, so don't bother looking. Also be sure not to confuse neutral grain spirits with denatured alcohol. The latter contains brucine, an alkaloid which is added for the very purpose of rendering it undrinkable (thus avoiding the federal liquor tax on alcohol that is intended only for industrial applications). Aside from tasting awful, brucine is also poisonous, so denatured alcohol is never to be consumed for any reason.

45 ml.	Vodka
15 ml.	Rum, light
15 ml.	Cointreau
3/4 teaspoon	Orange Zest - see directions below
3/4 teaspoon	Lime Zest - see directions below
15 ml.	Orange juice, fresh
15 ml.	Lime juice, fresh

Put the citrus zests into a fine mesh sieve, then slowly pour the orange and lime juices, then the vodka, rum, and Cointreau over the zest. Rub the zest in the strainer to get out as much liquid as possible, then the discard the zest. Add:

1 teaspoon	Maple Syrup
1 teaspoon	Pomegranate Syrup, homemade (page 79) or substitute Grenadine (not as good)

Shake with ice and strain into an ice cold chilled martini glass. Then float:

1 teaspoon   Gin, preferably a high-proof gin

This is a superb example of the supercharging effect. If this is your first exposure to supercharged citrus, it will be a true awakening.

Maxine's Slot Machine

My grandfather remarried a woman named Maxine, who was a generation or two younger than himself. I adored her, but then Maxine's bubbly positive personality was adorable to almost everyone, and her enthusiasm for gin cocktails and slot machines was legendary. This gin drink with the slot machine fruits of cherry, orange and lime is her legacy. Because of the color of this drink, she likened this to looking at the world through a rose colored glass.

50 ml.   Gin, London Dry
30 ml.   Cherry Brandy (liqueur), Marie Brizard
15 ml.   Grand Marnier
$^{3}/_{4}$ teaspoon   Orange Zest - see directions below
30 ml.   Lime juice, fresh

Grate the orange zest onto a fine mesh sieve and pour over the spirits one by one, then press the zest against the sieve to extract the last few drops. Discard the zest. Add the lime juice and shake with ice. Pour into a chilled tumbler along with the ice cubes, and garnish with a spear of fresh lime, orange and a maraschino cherry.

It is surprising to most bartenders today that many vintage cocktails relied on the zest of citrus without any of the actual juice of the fruit. For instance, the very popular *Liberty* cocktail of the 1920's consisted of pouring equal portions of sweet Italian vermouth and gin over the grated zest of a whole orange. This is an interesting cocktail, and should be prepared as a learning experience, if nothing else.

There are many cocktails in this book that call for the zest of a citrus fruit. This is almost never seen in commercial restaurants and bars now. This is only practical at home, or in top notch places with very high prices. Very few restaurants and bars operate that way today.

CUSTOMIZING LIQUORS

The technique of SUPERCHARGING citrus is related to the approach employed in *spiking* and *dousing*. By no means is the idea of secretly altering basic ingredients limited to citrus juices. Liquors such as rum contain complex flavors all by themselves. These flavor profiles can be easily manipulated by mixing brands together, and by the addition of flavoring components to infuse "mother liquors" used to formulate blends. *Dousing* refers to a small addition of a liqueur or bitter to a large volume of spirit, such as a few drops of absinthe mixed into an entire bottle of gin. Another favorite is the addition of a teaspoon or so of Grand Marnier into a bottle of cognac or rum. The effect is intentionally subtle.

Spiking is accomplished by the addition of pieces of dried fruit, spices, flowers, herbs, and other components to a bottle, and letting it steep for anywhere from a few hours to several weeks. After the flavors has sufficiently "developed" (like a photograph developing), the liquor is strained from the solids and moved to a clean bottle. It is important to remove the solid materials in order to stabilize the batch. Otherwise as time goes by, different materials will continue to add more and more flavor, while other components will have already given up everything they had to offer. The balance will change as time passes. Only by experimentation can you decide what you prefer in a blend, and how to get there.

The resulting mixture may be blended with other batches, or used directly. Recipes for the manipulation of liquors are usually closely guarded secrets. In fact, the very process itself is generally denied vehemently. In this way mixology is similar to magic. A good magician never reveals how he does a trick. The bartender appears to be pouring the same liquors you can buy anywhere, and yet produces a drink that you can not duplicate. The patron is left mystified as to how this is possible.

Examples of components to add to rum:

Citrus peels (lemon, orange, lime, grapefruit)
Raisins
Dried Apricots
Bay Leaf
Cloves
Cinnamon Sticks
Nutmeg
Hibiscus Tea
Ginger Root

Examples of components to add to gin:

Juniper Berries
Citrus peels (lemon, orange, lime, grapefruit)
Cardamom Pods (white or green, but never black)
Chamomile Tea
Cumin Seeds
Coriander Seeds
White Peppercorns
Tarragon
Dill Pickle, well rinsed

Examples of components to add to whiskey:

Citrus peels (lemon, orange, lime, grapefruit)
Cherries, pitted
Black Peppercorns
Molasses
Cigars, crushed up—and sometimes even partially smoked!

According to a rare mixologist guide published in 1894, cigars were partially smoked before being used to spike whiskey. In the same book, another ingredient being used was ambergris. Ambergris comes from the liver of the sperm whale, and was common in old perfumes. The flavor is powerful, unique, and impossible to imitate. If you are curious, you can learn more (and even buy this rare commodity) from a New Zealand company selling it online at ambergris.co.nz

If you regard such methods as being dishonest, or even weird, you should know that the infusion of natural flavors is employed on a commercial scale as many liquors are manufactured. The most elementary example is wine. Traditionally it was aged in different kinds of oak barrels (sometimes charred / smoked) because the wood of the barrel adds flavor components, and absorbs harsh flavors. Today many wines are produced in stainless steel tanks and wooden planks and sawdust are added to contribute those same flavors. This practice has also been employed in the manufacture of cognac for a very long time. Steeping herbs, berries and other flavoring components with vodka is the formula for making gin. Most rum distilleries are secretive about their methods, but many are known to add citrus peel and burnt woods during aging, and undoubtedly there are other components that they keep secret.

There is no such thing as a recipe for the perfect blended liquor, because the end result will depend on what it is going to be served as part of, and your individual palate. Just know that when you modify a spirit, you are not violating any sacred principle. You are just putting your own signature on the product. A distillery aims at producing liquor that will appeal to a mass market, and they taste their product straight (no mixers). *Your* goal is to create a final unique cocktail that can not be easily copied. It is the difference between producing wall paper and producing a work of art.

SAMPLE PROCEDURE - RUM X

One blend that I find especially useful for tropical drinks begins with white rum with bits of orange peel, lime peel, dried apricots, pink peppercorns, sichuan peppercorns, and a very small amount of bay leaf, and cloves. Let it stand for about three days before decanting. It is impossible to state the exact amount of any of these ingredients, because it will depend on the nature of the rum, the sweetness of the fruit, the freshness of the peppercorns, and of course, personal preference. Just keep in mind that if the mixture is not flavored enough, you can allow it to stand for a bit longer. Remember that flavors do not infuse at the same rate, though. More time means different flavors will begin to show up. Sometimes that's good, but it will depend on what you are spiking it with. If it is too strongly flavored, then you can strain off the solids and dilute it back down with more of the original rum that was used. You will have to try this a few times to see what the results are, and to see how this affects the flavor of the final destination cocktail. Rum X is especially well suited to daiquiris. I keep a bottle of this behind the bar with a letter "X" written on the back of the label, and occasionally refer to it as *Rum X* in this book.

A word of advice here: *Do not attempt to create beautifully polished drinks by strongly flavoring cheap liquor in order to conceal its inferior nature.* The underlying structure and balance can not be fixed by the addition of good flavor on top of the harsh and acrid flavors inherent in cheap booze.

The question you may be wondering now is just what quality of a light rum should you begin with for spiking it to produce your own *Rum X*? Up until the middle of the 1990's, when it came to light rum your choice was generally limited to Bacardi, or something like, *Kaptain Kwality* (made to fit the budget limitations of a homeless wino). Ten Cane and a couple of other brands emerged with the first premium white rums that had been marketed in decades. Their success has been a wake up call to the rest of the distillery industry. You can expect more fine white rums on the market in the future. The bottom line is that you should use the best rum that you can afford, within reason. I wouldn't spike a rare old bottle that was decades old, but neither would I waste my time and effort on Kaptain Kwality's rotgut, either.

Proving the old adage that for every rule there is an exception, I should also say that allowing an inexpensive rum to steep over a substantial quantity of golden raisins for a day (or longer) and then decanting it carefully to leave the soaked raisins behind, will improve the resulting flavor by a considerable margin. The raisins absorb some of the harshness and contribute fruit and sweetness. So much sweetness that the amount of sugar (or syrup) in the recipe may have to be reduced a bit to compensate, actually. This works surprisingly well. Still, I put this trick in the category of an academic experiment. It is the sort of thing you might resort to if stranded in a remote place with limited quality ingredients available. The effect is still only an *improvement*. There is no real cure for cheap liquor. A drink made with inferior products will never hold a candle to the same drink made from the top shelf. Perhaps this seems obvious to you already, but I have seen many a modern cocktail book that assures readers that mediocre quality spirits are all that one should ever purchase to make cocktails with. If you ever wonder whether this is true, then mix up two identical cocktails; one using cheap liquor and the other using the best ingredients you can obtain. Compare the two drinks side by side and you will never question the importance of first rate spirits again.

Remember that the purpose of spiking and blending liquors is *not* to create a liqueur, or an eau de vie. Only enough flavoring material is introduced to slightly alter the flavor profile. It is then called a *fixed* rum. Fixed rum should still taste like rum, as fixed gin should taste like gin. Otherwise your final cocktail will be unrecognizable. Imagine mixing a *Zombie* with lemonade in place of rum. If you flavor your liquor too much, this is the sort of thing that you will end up with.

The spiking, dousing and blending of liquor is very much a matter of personal taste. For this reason, such modifications have generally not been explicitly stated in the recipes in this book, with the exception of *Rum X* in a couple of places.

I also encourage you to try your hand at blending your own rums. One of the rums that I use is Bacardi *Black*, which is already a blend of seven to nine different rums itself. I do not often use most of Bacardi's product line, and especially not their flavored rums, but *Black* has a very useful flavor, with heavy tones of espresso, chocolate and leather.

SAMPLE PROCEDURE - RUM Z

Try substituting this blended and doused rum in place of dark rum in recipes. This is an easy and quick blend to make — which is very unusual in the realm of fixed rums.

200 ml.	Rum, Bacardi *Black*
50 ml.	Rum, Appleton *Special*
10 ml.	Apricot Cognac, homemade (page 69)

20 ml.	Natural Brown Sugar Syrup (page 53)
15 ml.	Orange juice, fresh
2x2x^{1}/$_{2}$" piece	White Bread, fresh (crust removed)

Shake and allow to stand for a few minutes before passing through a fine mesh sieve. Discard the soaked bread without squeezing it out. The resulting mixture will be slightly cloudy. If you need it to be perfectly clear, then pass it through layers of cheesecloth.

A FEW WORDS ABOUT GIN

One of the lesser known truths about cocktails of the 1920's to 1930's is that they were usually based on gin, not rum. Rum had a terrible reputation for a long time, being considered the rotgut of its day. Good quality gin was readily available, but "fine rum" was almost an oxymoron. Liquor historians frequently credit Don the Beachcomber as the ambassador of quality rum, but America's love affair with rum can really be traced to the countless tourists who traveled to the resorts of Cuba until the embargo. Up until that time Cuba was like Las Vegas and Tijuana rolled into one, and rum flowed like water. Before that time, gin was the most popular choice of mixologists. Just look at the number of gin recipes in cocktail books published before the 1940's. If you go back before the 1920's, there is hardly a rum drink to be found.

Gin is a peculiar liquor in that the flavor components become significantly muted when it is very cold. This is why martinis are best stirred, not shaken—despite James Bond's preference. One of the strangest promotions I ever saw was Tanqueray offering a free martini shaker with their Tanqueray *Ten* gin in a boxed set. The very characteristics that make Tanqueray *Ten* such a magnificent gin are concealed after it has been shaken with ice. Gin becomes more like vodka when it gets very cold. Tropical drinks are usually shaken with ice. Therefore, your drinks will benefit from a quality gin that can withstand some extra chilling.

★ DOCTORED GIN ★

I primarily work with two types of gin at the bar. The first is Hendricks. The other is Beefeater that has been spiked upon arrival with about a dozen juniper berries and a few small pieces of lemon peel. This intensifies the gin flavor, and helps it to shine through the sugar and other ingredients in tropical drinks. This spiking does cause a slight yellow coloration in the liquor, but fortunately that yellow cast is rarely a problem. If it is, then stick to Hendricks.

The single strongest flavoring component of any gin is juniper, and dried juniper berries are fairly easy to find in gourmet markets. If you can get your hands on some of the herb known as angelica, then by all means add a sprig of that in to steep with the juniper. I let it stand for at least a week before using a new bottle. Two weeks is better. Strain off the liquor into a fresh bottle before using, otherwise as the amount of liquor in the bottle decreases with use, the flavor of the berries and lemon peel will become increasingly powerful in the remaining volume.

By doctoring liquors in this manner, you are aiming for an effect that is almost subliminal by the time it is in the finished drink. This is your chance to personalize liquor to your own liking, and add your own signature to every drink you prepare—even classic simple recipes.

It is important to add only a small amount of any agent so that you will have time to taste it as the flavor develops. If you put too much of any one thing in, the flavor will change quickly and you will not have a chance to find a good balance. A true connoisseur will introduce a little more of one component or another as the flavors are changing over a period of days, or even weeks. Keep testing the mixture and compare it with the unaltered version of the same liquor periodically. When you believe that you have arrived at a useful point, make a couple of different cocktails using both the original commercial brand and the new "designer" liquor. Compare the two. It was not unusual for mixologists to combine dozens of different brands of rums and numerous flavoring components stored over months, or even years, to create batches of liquors that they knew could not be duplicated by anyone else ever. This is the an important aspect of the lost art in mixology. Something that is not even well documented, let alone employed these days.

"MAD SCIENTIST" LIQUORS

With yet another rebirth of the cocktail—which seems to be a perpetual event—manufacturers have sought to capitalize on this with a vast array of products that I collectively refer to as Mad Scientist Liquors. These include things like X-Rated, Mascarade, Saffron Infused Gin, Mandarin Orange Vodka, Alizé Red Passion, *etc.* Unfortunately some of these have a synthetic taste, or aftertaste. In fact some of the newest flavors taste more like children's cough syrup. You wouldn't blend fine and expensive spirits with medicine, would you? Listen, if you want to mix a drink with French cognac, passion fruit and cranberry, do yourself a favor and mix *actual* French cognac, passion fruit and cranberry juices together. Common sense should tell you that this will maximize the quality.

Occasionally something new comes along that does actually have merit. These include Hypnotq, and a few of the newer citrus vodkas, particularly Hangar One's *Buddha's Hand* Vodka. They contain flavors that are nearly impossible to duplicate. I think of Hypnotq as a grapefruit liqueur.

Hangar One's *Buddha's Hand* is actually made from a variety of citrus fruit by the same name. The fruit is seldom seen in the United States, though well known in Asia. The zest is more often used than the fruit itself.

Among the best of the new vodkas is Belvedere's *Cytrus*. Grey Goose's *La Poire* Pear Vodka is also very worthwhile. I am particularly fond of the Pear Martini described later in this book (page 203).

Many flavored rums and vodkas have not been worthy of mention in recent years. Some are worse than just terrible, because whatever other ingredients they come into contact with are transformed into a plasticized drug trip of cloying artificial synthetic sweetness. The only categorical exception to this is coconut rum. DeKuyper's *Tropical Coconut* is great. Note that this is identical to DeKuyper's older product, *San Tropique® Coconut Rum*. Recently DeKuyper renamed several of their signature liqueurs. Even though the names changed, the quality of the product inside the bottle is absolutely identical to the same high standard as before.

APRICOT BRANDY & APRICOT COGNAC

Apricot Brandy is an ingredient that seems to have been lost in translation over the decades, just as there is similar confusion today regarding Triple Sec and Cherry Brandy (see pages 75 and 77). In the 1930's there were two distinct varieties of apricot brandy. One was the sweet version that is still marketed today. In fact, to the best of my knowledge, this sweet version is the *only* version commercially marketed today. Unfortunately, if you are trying to duplicate a recipe published before 1940 that calls for apricot brandy, you just might be making the drink all wrong. There used to be a French variety that was hardly sweet at all, and obviously produced entirely different cocktails. The best simulation of this style of apricot brandy that I have been able to achieve involves soaking chopped dried apricots in just enough brandy to cover them for at least a week, shaking occasionally. Two weeks would be better. Store the bottle in the refrigerator during this time. You may add a little brown sugar if the apricots are very tart, but remember that you are trying to avoid making a sweet liqueur here. If you wanted that, then you could just buy Hiram Walker's fine product. After the mixture has stood for the duration, strain off the liquid and press the apricots against the mesh of a sieve to squeeze out the juice. Put this liquor in a bottle and leave it in the refrigerator. In other recipes in this book, I will refer to this as APRICOT COGNAC.

Two good examples of the use of this version are from the legendary mixologist, Charles Baker, Jr., of the 1930's, which I now present here...

Grande Bretagne Cocktail

Hailed as one of the finest drinks of all time back in the 1930's. Yet almost no one has heard of it these days. It is very dry and differs from what most people expect from a cocktail in our time. It is an interesting glimpse into what people liked back then. In case you don't know, Bretagne (also known as Brittany) is the western region of France.

45 ml.	Gin, Beefeater (doctored - page 65)
15 ml.	Apricot Cognac, made as described above
15 ml.	Lime, fresh juice
2-3 drops	Angostura Bitters
1 teaspoon	Egg White

Shake vigorously with ice and strain into a chilled martini glass. The common mistake made with this drink is to use the modern version of apricot brandy which is very sweet. This drink is not supposed to be sweet at all.

<u>Flying Fish</u>

This is based on one of Charles Baker, Jr.'s own personal favorites. This recipe differs slightly from his 1939 book, but he personally suggested a modification similar to that made here. I have tried both and I think it is safe to say that almost anyone these days would prefer this version. The main problem with this drink as far as I am concerned is that it is rather heavy. This was a style of the 1930's that once again shows how tastes have changed.

30 ml.	Gin, such as Bombay *Sapphire*
30 ml.	Apricot Cognac, made as described above
30 ml.	Marie Brizard *Peche du Verger*
8-10 drops	Peach bitters, Fee Bros.

Shake with ice and strain into a chilled martini glass.

<u>Sailfin</u>

This relative of the Flying Fish is more in keeping with taste trends today. Incidentally, *Sailfin* is a fine dining restaurant on the island of Bali. This drink may also be prepared with an unflavored vodka by adding a teaspoon of lime juice and a small piece of lime peel, but I suggest using Belvedere's *Cytrus* for the best results.

60 ml.	Citrus Vodka, ideally Belvedere *Cytrus*
15 ml.	Marie Brizard *Peche du Verger*

1 teaspoon	Apricot Cognac, made as described above
¹/₂ teaspoon	Pomegranate Syrup (page 79)
	or substitute Grenadine
4-5 drops	Peach bitters, Fee Bros.

Shake with ice and strain into a chilled martini glass.

☗

Tastes have certainly changed. What pleased every customer decades ago is often perceived as tasting like nasty medicine these days. Not very long ago a *Martini* was still being mixed with equal parts of gin and vermouth. Going back still further, a Martini also included sweet vermouth. This is just a simple example. My point is that even if you manage to perform the miracle of concocting a drink exactly the way that it would have tasted in another age, the result may be mostly of historical interest, when honestly evaluated.

Throughout this book the recipes nearly all specify a particular liquor brand and variety for each ingredient. This is a deviation from the norm of specifying only the type of liquor. This eliminates any guess work on your part of what the drink was supposed to taste like—a common problem in most recipes.

Another distinct difference in many of these recipes is the amount of alcohol contained. This may not be something you have paid particular attention to, but in most recipes the alcohol is generally kept to less than 2 ½ ounces (75ml). First, because most cocktail recipes originated in bars where profit is the first consideration, and mixers and sugar are a lot cheaper than liquor. Over the years, customers have gradually been weaned from the high-octane drinks that were the norm of the 1940's. These days a typical American patron is perfectly content with a cocktail that contains less than an ounce of actual liquor. Almost no complaints ever arise over drinks that contain 1 ½ ounces (45ml) of liquor, which is about half of the amount that was being poured in 1950.

Second, these days there is an increased concern by bartenders for legal trouble in getting a customer drunk. Many states actually have laws regulating the amount of liquor that can go into a single cocktail, and even hold the bartender criminally responsible for an intoxicated patron.

The problem is that there is simply no practical way to mix a very complicated drink without exceeding two ounces of liquor. The smaller the measurement you are using, the greater the error will be in measuring. If the original recipe contained five or six ounces of liquor and had aliquots of a sixth of a teaspoon of an ingredient (a "dash"), is to be scaled down so that the total liquor is only two ounces, you would need a calculator and a calibrated digital laboratory pipette to be able to maintain the same proportion—with that dash now being 0.000277 liters per drink. This is just one of the reasons why complex recipes are rarely seen these days.

Another reason is the amount of time that it takes to mix a drink. Bartenders are being paid by the hour, and a business must watch every minute spent by food and drink preparers in order to maximize profits. In case you ever wondered, they actually *do* measure the amount of time it takes to prepare every item on the menu. Something that takes eight minutes to make has to sell for a lot more than something that can be prepared in two minutes. If very few clients at that location would be willing to pay for that extra effort, then it won't be offered. It isn't worth training bartenders how to mix drinks that will rarely be ordered. That is the theory, anyway.

These factors explain why the true art of mixology is now largely history, except at the most expensive establishments in the world. There are bars in places like Tokyo and Beverly Hills that charge hundreds of dollars per cocktail. They make their own syrups using fresh ingredients. They use only super-premium spirits, and with the price of the drink being so high they can actually pay a bartender to devote six to eight minutes to preparing a single cocktail.

The only real problem with becoming proficient at making first rate cocktails is that you will never again be happy with what you are served at most commercial establishments.

KEY INGREDIENTS

<u>TRIPLE SEC</u>

This is a common cocktail ingredient that has been lost in translation over the decades. Most bartenders today assume that Triple Sec couldn't mean anything other than the clear white liqueur sold in every liquor store, and most grocery stores. It has a lot of sugar and some orange flavor, but it is almost undrinkable in its pure state to any discerning palate. Long ago, triple sec was a generic term for any orange liqueur that contained the peel of the orange, and was strictly regarded as a cheap substitute for Cointreau. Thus, any recipe that calls for Triple Sec is improved by substituting Cointreau, or in most cases any other intense orange liqueur. Examples include Grand Marnier, Harlequin, Marie Brizard's Orange Curaçao, *etc.* The specific choice of which orange liqueur is used is left up to the mixologist. Triple Sec was originally marketed to bars trying to increase profits. If you trying to produce high quality cocktails, you have absolutely no use for Triple Sec.

Sometimes one sees reference made to *Parfait Amour* liqueur, which is still produced by Marie Brizard (available online, but very rare to find in any liquor store). This is a blend of oranges from Spain, orange blossoms and vanilla bean pods distilled in some carefully controlled secret manner. It is an excellent liqueur to use in place of triple sec or orange curaçao in tropical drink recipes, but it will alter the color and the flavor of the final drink. Sometimes it is an improvement, and other times it is not. You have to see what you like personally on a case by case basis.

<u>BITTERS</u>

One of the most frequently misused components of a cocktail are aromatic bitters, such as Angostura. These are extremely powerful flavoring agents, and adding "two shakes" of Angostura to just about anything will leave it tasting more of the bitters than anything else. Also, this antiquated measurement of a "shake" is hopelessly inaccurate for a component with the power of nitroglycerin in a drink. In practice a shake can dispense anywhere from about four and twelve drops.

Some bartenders get so used to putting bitters in their drinks that they add them liberally to everything. This was especially true a few decades ago, but today one tends to see the exact opposite problem in which bitters are left out of the recipe. Your mastery of both the type of bitters and the proper amount to employ for the drink being prepared is mandatory knowledge for the expert mixologist.

When it comes to the design of tropical drinks, the only general rule of thumb I can provide is to try adding about three drops of Angostura bitters for every ounce of pineapple juice used. These two flavors compliment each other in a powerful way. In fact, try an experiment in which you pour two shots of straight pineapple juice. Add this ratio of Angostura bitters to one of the shots, and give it a stir. Compare the flavors. If you increase the Angostura bitters, you will see what I meant about how the balance quickly goes from beautiful and sophisticated, to crude and toxic tasting.

KIRSCHWASSER & CHERRY BRANDY

Here is another example of an ingredient which confuses many amateur mixologists. What is more confusing is that two distinctly different types of liquors are bottled with the same name, both translated into English on the label as "Cherry Brandy." As if this isn't already confusing enough, there is also a Danish formula known as Cherry Heering, which is sometimes called Peter Heering, after the inventor.

Kirschwasser (also called simply Kirsch sometimes) has a higher alcohol content, and is not a sweet liqueur. There are numerous cherry brandies on the market which have much in common with children's cherry flavored cough syrup (remember the *Flaming Moe* drink from the Simpsons?) In my opinion there are only two cherry brandies worthy of mixing in a quality cocktail. Namely, the original *Cherry*

Heering from Denmark, and Marie Brizard's *Cherry Brandy*. Both are hard to find in American stores these days, and the Internet once again saves the day if you are fortunate enough to live in a state that allows mailing liquor. Otherwise you may find yourself doing what I did when I lived in the US: Making excursions to others states with larger liquor suppliers and bringing back boxes of assorted bottles personally in the trunk of my car. New York has the best suppliers there, but there are reasonably good sources in other large cities, too.

In between the extremes of the liter bottles of Kirschwasser found in discount liquor stores, and the very expensive handmade Austrian and German small batch imports, are the artisanal small-production types such as Black Star Farms "Spirit of Cherry" that I highly recommend. This is what I personally use for Kirschwasser, because the flavor is superb in cocktails and it is still affordable.

GRENADINE

Grenadine is supposed to be a pomegranate flavored syrup. It has became one of the most corrupted ingredients in all history. In most bottled versions today, it is almost synonymous with red-colored high-fructose corn syrup. There are a few super premium grade grenadines available that are better than the supermarket variety. In particular there is an organic grenadine that is produced in France which is delicious, but very hard to find. The only source I know of personally in the United States is in the Farmer's Market on Third Street in Los Angeles, in the French Market and restaurant at the east end of the pavillion. They tend to sell out of this grenadine days after they get new inventory, and it can be several months between shipments. It is *that* good! However, that is not to say that it is authentic. If you want the truly authentic experience, at least according to what was available in the 1930's on the high seas, you have only one option: Make it yourself. The result will be very different from anything you buy, and quite similar to the product bottled by Trader Vic in the 1960's as Pomegranate Syrup (originally not even called Grenadine by Vic).

<u>POMEGRANATE SYRUP</u>

Below is a recipe for pomegranate syrup that you should use in place of commercial grenadine when attempting to recreate any cocktail recipe dating before 1950, or just to improve the taste of any drink that calls for grenadine. It is astoundingly better than anything you can buy. Many people make the mistake of confusing "pomegranate molasses" with pomegranate syrup. They are very different. Pomegranate molasses is boiled with lemon juice, and cooked for a very long time which causes a lot of oxidation. The flavor is murky and caramelized, which is fine if you are using it in Middle Eastern cooking, which is what it is intended for. Do not even think about using it as a substitute for pomegranate syrup in a cocktail. You might as well add ketchup to your shaker for how it will taste. Having said that, of course there are a few rare recipes that actually do call for pomegranate molasses in a cocktail, but such a recipe will certainly call attention to this weird ingredient. One such cocktail in this book is *Red Mercury* (page 197).

First mix up a sugar solution containing a ratio of one cup of sugar to a cup of water. Slice two fresh pomegranates in half, and smack out the seeds using the back of a large wooden spoon. Put the seeds into a pan and add the sugar water solution, plus a splash of vodka. Bring to a boil, then reduce heat and keep at a simmer for 30 minutes uncovered. The evaporation during this stage will increase the sugar concentration. Stir occasionally during this time. After half an hour, turn off the heat and cover the pan. Let the mixture steep for about two hours as it cools. Put the entire contents into a food processor and let it run for about a minute. Pass the mixture through a sieve back into the pan, and bring to a boil. Reduce the volume to about a cup, stirring to make sure it does not burn at the bottom. Store the syrup in the refrigerator.

The following recipe showcases the quality of this homemade Pomegranate Syrup…

This is a surprisingly intense and curious drink. The name is taken from the bottle label on the shrinking potion described in *Alice in Wonderland*. Despite its bright pink color, this is not quite so much the "girl drink" that one would imagine. It is far less sweet than you would expect from the amount of syrup used and really showcases the power of the SUPERCHARGED citrus process. One reason that I like this recipe is that it is fairly simply, yet quite mysterious to the guest who tries to guess what it might possibly contain.

60 ml	Rum, light
10 ml.	Vodka
1 $^1/_2$ teaspoons	Grapefruit Zest - see directions below
15 ml.	Cherry Brandy (liqueur), Marie Brizard
	or substitute Cherry Heering
15 ml.	Lemon Juice, fresh
20 ml.	Pomegranate Syrup, homemade (see above)

Grate the zest onto a fine mesh sieve and pour the rum over it slowly. Then slowly drizzle the vodka over the same zest. Press the zest against the sieve to expel as much of the liquid as possible, then discard the zest. Combine with the rest of the ingredients and shake with ice. Strain into a chilled glass. Consider serving this in a clear bottle with a cork and a tag that reads "Drink Me!" hanging from the side. I like to supply a straw with the bottle, and nothing else.

Unless otherwise stated, this refers to a highly sweetened coconut syrup. Better bars employ *Coco Lopez* canned coconut cream, which is readily available in American supermarkets and liquor stores. I won't even mention the kind of things that worse bars use. I am concerned with what is best in this book, and to that end you should consider making up your own coconut cream. There is an acceptable shortcut that avoids you having to grate a mountain of fresh coconut pulp, thankfully. Buy unsweetened coconut milk, as used in Thai cooking (check your local supermarket). Then add half a cup of sugar per can of coconut, and bring it to a boil on the stove while stirring. When it is reduced by half in volume, let it cool before putting it into a jar and storing it in the refrigerator. The taste is not cloyingly sweet like the commercial canned product is, and the drinks it produces will have a much more refined taste—even a simple Pina Colada.

CITRUS JUICES

While the novice bartender and inferior establishment may rely on a bottle of sweet and sour mix, this is about as smart as having used rusty water to make your ice cubes with. To start with fine aged liquors and then mix them with a witch's brew of chemicals and artificial flavoring agents is the epitome of wastefulness. The "sweet and sour" component of any quality Tiki-style drink is strictly freshly squeezed citrus juice blended with some kind of syrup. There are a number of so-called "professional" bartending courses offered online, and by DVD these days in which the instructor reaches for a plastic bottle of sweet and sour mix frequently. This is because their instructions are aimed at people who will seek employment at commercial bars and restaurants, where the taste of the drink takes a back seat to the profit margin.

When it comes to orange juice, it has been my consistent experience in the United States that mandarin oranges yield the only acceptable fresh juice. The opposite is the case in Europe, where mandarin oranges often contain an odd aroma. If you are in Europe, then choose the kind of oranges that have patches of dark reddish skin on them. The name will depend on where you are at. I have never seen that variety in the United States, but they are the absolute best.

PINEAPPLE JUICE

Dole manufactures an excellent 100% pineapple juice in cans, although drinks that are very strongly pineapple-based will benefit from fresh juice. The lesson here is that over-ripe pineapple is best. You actually want pineapple that is on the verge of rotting, because it is sweeter and slightly alcoholic. Not to the point of having any fungal taste, mind you! This is not the prettiest pineapple, because it is often slightly brown, but the flavor of that juice is the best.

Something else worth noting about pineapple juice is that it oxidizes slightly when shaken. In many drinks this changes the flavor slightly. Even though I have not bothered to explicitly state this in any of the recipes here, you would be advised to experiment by shaking the ice with all of the ingredients *except* the pineapple juice first, and then gently stir in the pineapple juice called for in the recipe. Some drinks will benefit from this more than others. I didn't want to repeat this same message with every recipe in this book that calls for pineapple juice, so just keep this in mind as you proceed.

YUZU JUICE & YUZU EXTRACT

Yuzu is a Japanese citrus fruit that is somewhat like grapefruit and lemon, but has its own distinct flavor notes. Fresh Yuzu is hard to find outside of Asia, but there is a freeze dried variety that can be purchased in many Asian food stores in a sealed foil package. One such brand is the package shown to the right here. The best way to use this is to place the small bits from the package into a bottle containing just enough vodka to cover them, and then let

it stand for at least a week. A month is better, and two months wouldn't hurt. Then strain off the solids and use the resulting concentrated fluid sparingly. If you can obtain fresh yuzu, then so much the better. At least this method will allow you to incorporate the flavor notes of this exotic fruit in cocktails, as long as the yuzu is a minor component.

ICE

The unsung hero? …or is it the enemy of the cocktail? Not just the amount of ice, but what the ice is made of is of considerable importance. Most cocktails need to be chilled and *slightly* diluted. Far too many bars take this as an excuse to to shake half an ounce of liquor with two cups of ice so that the resulting drink costs as little as possible, and has nearly no flavor. There is no standard for to what constitutes the perfect proportion of ice and (hence) dilution. I can tell you that for most drinks I prefer to use the least amount of ice possible, and make up for it with a little extra shake or stir time. This maximizes the flavor intensity. However, people who only drink very occasionally will usually prefer a drink with more ice than liquor. Otherwise all they will taste is alcohol—and they will often tell you just that.

Some older cocktail recipe books would actually instruct you as to how many times to shake each drink, and exactly how much ice to add (*e.g.* half a cup of ice, shake eight times). For those who have absolutely no sense about how much ice or shaking is required, I suppose this sort of micromanagement is a good thing. I will trust in you to be able to use sensible judgement in the quantity of ice and duration of the shake. In a few instances I have specifically noted more or less ice than usual as a suggestion.

In some instances, the best result is actually obtained by preparing the drink ahead of time and storing it in the refrigerator. Then pour the prechilled mixture over ice cubes (or straight up, if you want to really concentrate the flavor) into a chilled glass. If you happen to have a drink that includes pieces of fruit in it, then this is especially good, because the chilled fruit will act like ice cubes that do not dilute the drink.

You can also make up specialized ice cubes for specific drinks. This has became somewhat common lately for Dirty Martinis in the most expensive establishments, in which the ice cubes are actually frozen brine from the olives. An even more devious approach is to make a batch of whatever drink you plan to serve, and pouring it into an ice cube tray. Then when you mix that same drink fresh, use those ice cubes of the same drink to chill it down. No matter how long someone takes sipping their drink, there will be no loss in flavor. Just know that ice cubes containing a lot of alcohol will need a very cold freezer to become solid, and it will take a while.

Of course, if you like your drinks watered down more, then this approach is not going to please you. Personally I like a drink that has a serious kick to it, and too much water from the melted ice dampens the flavor. Many of the drinks that I serve are prepared several hours ahead of time and stored in the refrigerator, then poured straight up in a glass that has been stored in the freezer. This is something you have to try a few times. One warning though: Once you get used to this level of intense flavor, you will be disappointed with almost any drink you are served in a restaurant or bar.

When it comes to regular ice, be sure to use distilled water, or at least filtered water. It is quite ridiculous to pay for the best quality spirits only to have them corrupted by ice melting into the drink that is slightly metallic, or has a hint of foul odor. If you are operating a commercial establishment, be aware that the taste of your local water may seem completely neutral to you if you grew up in that region, while a visitor from another country, or even another part of the same state may find your water horribly distasteful. I have had this experience many times in my travels. One example is the water in Anaheim, California. It always tastes like chlorinated sewage to me. Yet locals swear they don't taste anything in it. Unless you are certain of how pristine your local water supply is, spend the money for distilled water. It is still the least expensive ingredient in any cocktail.

‟ <u>OTHER SYRUPS</u> „

Aside from Grenadine (previously described on page 78), the nature of other syrups used in cordials and cocktails are frequently overlooked as a vital factor in determining the quality of the cocktail being prepared. While there is some personal satisfaction in preparing your own syrups, putting one's ego aside, a lot of commercially prepared syrups are of excellent quality. I am particularly fond of Torani's line. Some of Monin's are also very good. Certain desirable flavors, such as starfruit, are not commercially available.

One problem with commercial syrups today is that many are made from high-fructose corn syrup instead of cane sugar. It is a tragedy to mix expensive, highly refined and aged liquors with syrup that wouldn't even make a good soda pop. When the amount of syrup is small in proportion to the other ingredients, then you can get away with second rate commercial products. But the drink will never be at its best—which, after all, is the single goal of the *art* of mixology. Making your own syrups is not difficult. The rule of thumb in almost all of syrups from about 1890 through 1960 was a fixed ratio of two pounds of cane sugar to each pint of liquid (water and juice being counted together). Keep this in mind when trying to recreate authentic flavors. Before 1890 there was more variation. After 1960, high fructose corn syrup started to gain popularity with manufacturers.

ORGEAT SYRUP

Arguably, the single most important syrup in tropical drinks is Orgeat, which is based on almonds and sugar. Originally it also contained barley, and was used in pharmaceutical preparations during the 18th century. The barley component is unpleasant tasting in cocktails and was dropped long ago. I find that the Orgeat made by both Monin and Torani is unacceptable for cocktails. Both have an odd synthetic aftertaste, which is strange since they claim to employ only natural almond flavor. Fee Brothers, who generally make outstanding products, are also very disappointing in their Orgeat Syrup.

Trader Vic's is the only commercial brand of Orgeat syrup that I would recommend. Beachbum Berry has said the same thing in his books. Trader Vic had been using French Garier Orgeat back in the 1940's. As far as I know, this outstanding product was discontinued long ago. He formulated his own replacement orgeat, and really created a masterpiece. It is ironic because Trader Vic's Orgeat contains a long list of synthetic ingredients that seem to have no business being there ideally, but the overall taste is so good that one can hardly believe it is a mixture of high fructose corn syrup, ester of wood rosin, brominated vegetable oil, propylene glycol, and artificial flavors. Sometimes its best not to read the label and just go by taste, which is simply the best product made.

That doesn't mean that it is authentic, though. I have never seen a commercially bottled Orgeat that contained only water, almonds and sugar. Probably because of the expense of it.

Generally speaking, use Trader Vic's Orgeat. It can be hard to find in liquor stores these days, but it is readily available from the source itself: tradervics.com (where you will also find recreations of great ceramic ware and glassware from the restaurant's historic past for sale).

Authentic homemade Orgeat syrup is different, and will produce distinctive cocktails, but it is far more expensive and will take some effort. As long as you are going to the trouble of making your own Orgeat, I suggest trying this dark version that includes the almond skins...

DARK ORGEAT SYRUP

Soak 450 grams of almonds (with their skin on) in enough distilled water to cover them. After 30 minutes drain them and discard this first liquid. Grind the almonds in a food processor. Do not process into a paste! You are looking for bread crumb consistency. Scrape the almond pulp back into a pan with 4 cups of water, 1 cup of sugar and 1 ounce of vodka. Bring to a gentle boil, then reduce heat and let it simmer for 30 minutes uncovered. Turn off the heat and cover it. Let the pan stand until it is room temperature. This will take several hours.

Next, pass the mixture through a food mill, or coarse strainer. Then put it back into the rinsed out pan, and reduce further on a high heat until down to 10 ounces (1 $^1/_4$ cups) in volume. Pass this through a fine sieve. Then again through a chinois, or "china cap" (ultra fine mesh sieve) or several layers of cheesecloth. The cheesecloth will cost you some of the syrup, though - it soaks into the cloth. A very fine mesh strainer won't lose any product, but such strainers are somewhat expensive. Finally add about a teaspoon of Grand Marnier. Traditionally orgeat included orange flower water, but a touch of Grand Marnier will work nicely.

The resulting syrup is stored in the refrigerator. It is brown in color and will create a milky color in any drink it is used in. The flavor is deep and pure. Some cocktails really benefit from this homemade syrup. Here is an example...

<u>Mahiki Tiki</u>

75 ml.	Mahiki *Cognac Cask Rum* (Barbados)
1 teaspoon	Grand Marnier
20 ml.	Lemon juice, fresh
20 ml.	Orange juice, fresh
$^1/_2$ teaspoon	Orange Zest - see directions below
15 ml.	Orgeat Syrup, dark homemade - see above
2-5 drops	Complexing Agent #1 (page 240)

Place the orange zest in a fine mesh sieve and pour the fresh orange and lemon juices over the zest. Discard the zest. Combine the rest of the ingredients. Shake with ice and serve on the rocks in a chilled glass with a straw, and garnish with a piece of fresh and very ripe pineapple. The drink will be milky due to the homemade orgeat.

Aztek-tini

There is a touch of whimsy here with bitter cocoa replacing the Angostura bitters commonly used in the traditional Aztek cocktail. Angostura overpowers the delicate flavor of the dark orgeat here, and cocoa adds wonderful depth and character, on an almost subliminal level. The homemade orgeat–while seemingly only a fractional component–lifts this drink up from the ordinary to the extraordinary. I got the idea of substituting cocoa powder for the Angostura bitters after noticing the similarity between the Aztek Cocktail and the Carlton St. Moritz cocktail that I had previously created (page 184), plus the idea of a Mexican theme drink with a subtle note of chocolate made perfect sense.

60 ml.	Tequila, Cazadores *Reposado*
30 ml.	Grapefruit Juice, fresh
15 ml.	Orgeat, dark homemade
15 ml.	Grand Marnier
pinch	Cocoa powder (99% cacao)
pinch	Cinnamon powder

Shake with ice and serve either on the rocks, or straight up. I prefer the latter, but this is often overpowering for those used to the typical watered-down restaurant drink strength.

Easter Island Cocktail

This drink is a cousin of the *Christmas Island* cocktail described in a later section. It was first created when living abroad where some of the ingredients of the Christmas Island cocktail were unavailable. This is an impressive drink that proves that more ingredients can produce a drink with beautiful layers of flavor, and not merely a muddled mess, as the old conventional wisdom predicted.

60 ml	Cognac
20 ml	Coconut Rum, DeKuyper *Tropical Coconut*
10 ml	Grand Marnier
1 teaspoon	Apricot Cognac (page 69)
30 ml	Lemon Juice, fresh
20 ml	Pineapple Juice
15 ml	Orgeat, dark homemade
pinch	Cardamom, ground
2-3 drops	Angostura bitters

Shake with ice. This drink was originally served on the rocks with a straw in an Easter Island statue shaped tall glass, but it is also fine sipping straight up from a chilled glass with a straw. It may be a cliché, but I prefer the maraschino cherry and pineapple garnish on this drink.

<u>ORANGE-ALMOND SYRUP</u>

This is prepared in nearly the same way as the Dark Orgeat Syrup previously described, with the following changes: First, almonds with no skin on them are generally preferred (but not mandatory). Second, add the zest of three medium size oranges to the almonds at the stage when they are to be ground up in the food processor. Even better, use the zest of one to two oranges plus $^{1}/_{2}$ teaspoon of orange oil (available at gourmet kitchen supply stores). Follow the rest of the procedure just as described for the Dark Orgeat.

<u>Easter Mai Tai</u>

This is close to the original 1944 Trader Vic formula. The Appleton Estate Jamaica Rum specified here is actually made under supervision of Wray & Nephew, who made the rum in the original drink from that era. Crème de Noyaux is not part of the original Mai Tai recipe, but it plays part of the role of the Orgeat, and adds some other interesting complexity.

60 ml.	Rum, Appleton Estate Jamaica 21 year old
15 ml.	Cointreau
15 ml.	Lime juice, fresh
10 ml.	Orange-Almond Syrup (see above)
1 teaspoon	Crème de Noyaux

Shake with ice and serve on the rocks in a chilled tumbler.

YELLOW PERSIMMON SYRUP

This syrup adds an astringent taste to any drink, and must be used sparingly. A teaspoon full is usually enough for any drink. The effect is so extreme that it is something that you really must experience personally to fully appreciate. Yellow Persimmon Syrup is one of those ingredients that was known to expert mixologists a long time ago, but seldom mentioned in writing. The only book that I have ever found that explained it in detail is, *Master Mixology* by "Charles" published privately in 1905, as a 38 page pamphlet. Try a *little* added to any drink that uses lemon-lime soda as a mixer, because it helps tame the taste introduced by the high-fructose corn syrup and artificial flavorings.

Mix up a solution of 1 ¼ cups sugar and 1 ¼ cups water in a sauce pan. Trim and coarsely chop five to six persimmons (not yet fully ripe) and add to the sugar water in the pan. Bring to a boil, then cover and simmer about 40 minutes. Let it cool, then put in a food processor and mince to a pulp. Pass this through a medium-fine screen with a food mill. Reduce this to about 1 cup, then filter through a fine sieve. Bottle and store in the refrigerator.

It is important to select fruit that is not fully ripe (yellow with some orange tones - but not bright orange), or you will not obtain the correct tannic flavor.

Okinawa Corker

This drink is not sweet. It was named after one of the most legendary storms in maritime history, which struck in the middle of World War II. The storm was so severe that it actually sank US Navy destroyers, along with many merchant ships. My father was on a ship during the storm, and recalled waves a hundred feet above the deck of the ship. When the storm had ended, one of the steel ladders on the deck of the ship had been twisted into a corkscrew shape by the velocity of the wind.

Blue Curaçao was rarely seen in those days, and so it was made up with blue food coloring and Cointreau. In reality, the homemade Blue Curaçao worked a lot better for three reasons. First, because it would have so much more food coloring in it than the commercial Blue Curaçao you buy (to the point of it being dark navy blue). Second, because the Blue Curaçao you make yourself does not immediately sink to the bottom of the drink, so the visual effect is better. Third, Cointreau just tastes better than Triple Sec. You *can* use the commercial bottled Blue Curaçao, but it won't be quite the same.

50 ml.	Rum, light
15 ml.	Lemon juice, fresh
3/4 teaspoon	Yellow Persimmon Syrup (page 95)

$^1/_2$ teaspoon	Monin *Curaçao Triple Sec* syrup
	or substitute simple syrup (not as good)
1 teaspoon	Blue Curaçao - see notes above

Mix the above ingredients (except Blue Curaçao) with fine cracked ice and shake. Pour the mixture (including the chipped ice) into a chilled highball glass with a straw. Float the Blue Curaçao. Note that if you are using the commercial variety, most of it will sink to the bottom of the drink.

Persimmon Martini

Try adding between one-fourth and one-half teaspoon of Yellow Persimmon Syrup to your next Martini, along with the usual gin and vermouth. Those who like a very dry martini will be surprised by just *how* dry this is. The syrup also adds a slight cloudiness, which is a lovely touch to a shaken Martini that adds the illusion of it being even colder than it is. If you like this taste, and serve a lot of martinis, consider flavoring an entire bottle of gin at a time. Put a small mark on the label to remind yourself that this is "martini gin" only. Guests are inclined ask what exotic and unusual brand of gin you used, but no one will ever guess persimmon flavor.

GUAVA PASTE

A number of 1950-1960's cocktail recipe call for guava nectar. This was usually interpreted as the canned variety, such as that produced and marketed by Kerns. In the South

Pacific, canned exotic juices were scarce in the 1940's, but fresh fruits were available. These were turned into a paste that was dished out by the teaspoon (that being about 5 ml) since it is too thick to pour easily. Guava fruit is hard to find in many parts of the world, in which case your only option will be to substitute a mixture of applesauce and canned guava juice. If you are absolutely stuck, you can use simply applesauce. I implore you to make every effort to use the original guava paste recipe below. The results are worth it.

Wash the fruit. For each guava (weight is about 4 $^1/_2$ ounces on average) trim off the stem end, then coarsely chop the fruit up (including the skin). Put them into a heavy bottomed pot with enough water to cover and 4 tablespoons of sugar per whole fruit. Bring to a boil, then reduce heat to a simmer for one hour. Stir occasionally to help break up the fruit. When the time is up, remove from heat and let it cool for a few minutes. Puree in a blender, then pass through a fine sieve, using the back of a rubber spatula to scrape through as much of the pulp as possible. Store in the refrigerator.

TAMARILLO SYRUP

The tamarillo is somewhat astringent with bitter properties that produces some interesting cocktails. It plays especially well with Campari. The tamarillo used to be called the tree tomato. Tamarillo fruit is available in high end grocery stores from time to time.

Remove the stem from each fruit and discard. Slice the fruit into large pieces and weigh them. Place the chunks in a heavy sauce pan with an equal volume of water (*e.g.* 4 ounces of fruit gets 4 ounces of water). Add one tablespoon of unprocessed sugar (or light brown sugar) per ounce of fruit. Note that this is not a typical syrup, as the sugar concentration is much lower than the standard amount. The sugar here is only really enough to offset the sour nature of the fruit. Keep this mixture just below boiling (slow simmer) for about 15 minutes, while you mash the fruit pieces with the back of a fork. You will find that much of the flesh seems to have dissolved by the end of that time. Strain through a fine sieve, using a rubber spatula to push as much through as you can, and to scrape the bottom of the sieve to release the sticky mass that didn't drop off of the sieve. Bottle this and store in the refrigerator. It should be stored for a full day before using it, as the flavor improves quite a lot during cooling and initial storage.

Original Armadillo

The name is based on a concatenation of the Armenian cognac and tamarillo syrup. While most of the recipes supplied in this book are too sweet to be considered an aperitif, this is one exception. The Armadillo is especially delicious before Cuban food, or spicy Italian food with a tomato-based sauce.

75 ml.	Armenian Cognac
	or substitute another cognac
15 ml.	Tamarillo Syrup - see above
10 ml.	Lemon juice, fresh
1 teaspoon	Campari

Swirl the tamarillo syrup and lemon juice with the Campari at the bottom of a shaker. Add a few ice cubes and pour cognac over. Stir to mix gently. Do not shake. This will keep it clear with golden red hues. Decant from the ice cubes into a glass, or split into several shotglasses. Note that this drink is almost universally appreciated by Europeans, but not always by Americans, who tend to prefer weaker and sweeter cocktails.

PASSION FRUIT SYRUP

Fee Brothers makes an acceptable product, but you will never achieve the best results possible with any commercial passion fruit syrup. You should definitely try making your own at least once to see the difference.

Combine ¾ cup sugar, ¾ cup water, and the scooped out pulp of 10 passion fruits in a heavy-bottom pan. Bring to a boil, then reduce to a simmer for ten minutes. Place a lid on the pan and allow it to cool off for fifteen minutes (off the heat). Puree in a food processor for at least a full minute. Pass through a fine sieve, using a rubber spatula to scrape the sides of the sieve and collect as much as possible, but leaving all of the black seeds behind. Bring this strained puree to a rapid boil and reduce until the volume is 1 cup. Bottle and store in the refrigerator.

STARFRUIT SYRUP

This is one of the most useful flavors in tropical drinks, and must be prepared yourself. Fortunately this is easy. Trim the ends off of a starfruit, then slice the rest of the fruit into very thin slices. Put this in a pan with enough simple syrup (equal parts sugar and water) to cover the fruit. Bring to a gentle boil and then reduce heat to a simmer for about 15 minutes. Put the entire contents into a jar and store in the refrigerator. The thin slices of fruit will continue to flavor the liquid some as time goes by, and they can also be taken out and used as a garnish, as in the case of the *Starfruit Martini* (see recipe on page 204).

LYCHEE SYRUP

Torani produced the absolute best Lychee Syrup that I have ever tried. Unfortunately it seems to have been discontinued by their company, at least at the time of this writing. Do not substitute Monin's Lychee Syrup. My personal experience with this flavor of theirs has been terrible and it had a bad aftertaste, to boot. If you have a large Asian supermarket near you (there are some in Los Angeles and New York City, especially) then you might be able to purchase a Chinese Lychee Syrup. The bottle is labeled entirely in Chinese, so you will need the help of a store employee, or a bilingual friend to try to locate it. Some of the Korean products are also very good, but considerably harder to find outside of Korea.

There is a *Creme de Lychee* manufactured in France by Gabriel Boudier. It is an interesting liqueur in its own right,

but it lacks the flavor intensity and the sweetness of the former Torani syrup. A "quick and dirty" approach to producing Lychee Syrup is to mix some of Boudier's *Creme de Lychee* with sugar in the ratio of 3 parts liqueur to 2 parts of sugar. Heat it up to get the sugar to dissolve. You can use a microwave oven for this if you are careful, but don't let it boil. You only want to heat it barely enough to dissolve the sugar completely. The resulting solution can be regarded as Lychee Syrup for the purpose of mixing drinks. It works very well in most drinks. Of course this assumes that you can obtain *Creme de Lychee*, which could mean shopping online, depending on where you live.

In case you are thinking of using the packing syrup from a can of lychees, forget it. That liquid contains preservatives you don't want, and very little actual lychee flavor. However with some effort you can produce an even better Lychee Syrup using the canned lychees themselves, which are available in most large supermarkets in the Asian foods aisle, as well as in any Asian market. Drain them first (discard the liquid), then puree them with equal parts of sugar and water. Put the resulting slurry into a heavy-bottom pan and bring to a slow boil on the stove. Let it simmer for about 15 minutes. Allow it to cool for another 15 minutes, then strain through a fine mesh sieve. Now bring to a boil again to evaporate more of the water. The exact amount will depend slightly on the brand of lychees you purchased (some are better than others). I should caution you that if you attempt to reduce the syrup down too much, it will begin to caramelize, and the delicate flavor will be destroyed. The commercial high-vacuum distillation method used by Torani is not something you can do at home. Also, I have experimented with both canned and fresh lychees, and a mixture of the two produced the best results, but you will probably have difficulty finding fresh lychees.

As a final note here, be sure to try the *Lychee Martini* described later in this book (page 199).

MANGO SYRUP

The quality of Fee Bros. is superb and it is produced using a method that can not be duplicated at home. Unfortunately there have been times when this was simply impossible to obtain, particularly in Eastern Europe. After some experimentation, the best result I could obtain was as follows:

Although fresh mangos would work best, in the instances when I could not obtain mango syrup, I could also not find fresh mangos, so I provide the details of this based on canned fruit. Drain one regular size can of mangoes to get rid of the nasty packing liquid (and as in the case of Lychee Syrup stated above, don't even think about using the packing syrup from the can). Break up the fruit with the back of a fork—or better yet, puree the fruit in a food processor, and put them into a heavy pot with 1/2 cup of sugar and 3/4 cup of water. Bring to a boil and then simmer for a few minutes to ensure that the sugar has all dissolved. Strain this through a fine mesh, scraping the sieve to make sure that as much of the solids pass through as possible. Put this solution into a heavy-bottom pan and boil to reduce it down to about half of its volume - perhaps more. You will need to taste it as it gets closer and watch out for signs that it is starting to burn, which must be avoided. Stir it often as it reduces. Commercially bottled products are distilled under high vacuum, which keeps the highly-volatile aldehydes that are responsible for the subtle flavors from oxidizing during the distillation. Vacuum distillation is impossible at home, unfortunately. As a result, the flavor of homemade mango syrup will never be as good as the commercial variety. It is also quite thick after it cools, and thus somewhat difficult to measure.

In general, if at all possible, just stick to purchasing Fee Bros. Mango Syrup. This will probably mean an online purchase, as very few liquor stores actually stock this particular syrup on their shelves. One final note: Mango syrup plays especially well with Jamaican rums.

<u>North Market Mango Cocktail</u>

This is an example of a cocktail that is made with the homebrew mango syrup just described. This drink was named in tribute to one of the best gourmet grocery stores in St. Petersburg, Russia, from which the ingredients for this cocktail were gathered late one night in haste as I was called upon to prepare a degustation menu of lamb, in the style of *Iron Chef*. I wanted a cocktail that would compliment a mild Punjabi style lamb curry, slowly cooked with tomatoes and cream. This was created with the Russian palate in mind, using two of their favorite flavors in an unexpected way. Namely black pepper and sugar. Vinjak is very similar to cognac, but it has notes of black pepper. This has been further bolstered here by adding actual peppercorns. For more about

Vinjak, see page 220.

60 ml.	Jamaican Rum, Appleton *Special*
30 ml.	Vinjak, Cezar - see note above or substitute cognac
$^1/_2$ teaspoon	Black Peppercorns, whole - see below
30 ml.	Pineapple juice
30 ml.	Lime juice, fresh
30 ml.	Mango Syrup, homemade - see above
$^1/_4$ teaspoon	Black Balsam (see page 222) or substitute 2-3 drops Angostura bitters (better)

Prepare ahead: For each ounce of Vinjak (or cognac) put about half a teaspoon of whole black peppercorns together with it in a jar and close it up. Let it steep for 20-30 minutes, shaking occasionally. Prepare the garnish during this same time (read below).

Combine all of the ingredients and shake with ice cubes. Pour the contents (including the ice) into a chilled highball glass with a straw. Garnish with a canned mango slice that has been soaked in Vinjak (or cognac) for at least 15 minutes before, or better yet, for several hours.

<u>SPICED SYRUP</u>

This simple recipe will enable you to produce your own outstanding spiced rum for cocktails, as well as being useful in flavoring cocktails that do not even contain rum.

Multiply the ingredients to obtain the amount you want to prepare. Lightly toast fennel seeds in a cast iron pan. Do not burn them. Transfer these to a mortar and pestle (or a spice grinder). For each teaspoon of seeds that you just toasted, add 5 whole cloves. Grind to a coarse powder. Put this powder into a pan on the stove. For each teaspoon of seeds you started with, add 1/4 cup (60 ml) of water and 2 tablespoons (25 grams) of brown sugar. Bring to a boil and let it continue boiling for 5 minutes. Filter this through a cone of paper towel in a funnel. If you are going to be doing this a lot then consider purchasing a Buchner funnel from a laboratory supply store, and box of Whatman #1 filter paper the right size for the funnel. Wet the paper first to keep solids from escaping around the edges into the filtrate.

GOMME SYRUP

This is an ingredient that you find mentioned often in old cocktail books. It is simply sugar syrup with the addition of a little gum arabic, which acts to keep the sugar from crystalizing out around the edges as it is stored. Because gum arabic is also an emulsifying agent, it will help blend and stabilize a cocktail that calls for drops of a flavored oil (such as neroli oil). There are very few examples of such drinks, though. Otherwise you should replace gomme syrup with simple sugar syrup (two parts sugar to one part water).

Making your own syrups may be personally rewarding, but it does not *always* lead to the best cocktail. The mango syrup previously described is an example of this (see text above). In some instances, such as the Yellow Persimmon Syrup, there is simply no choice but to make it yourself, because it is not produced commercially. Sometimes the commercially available product is of such poor quality that it can not be used. Other times you must accept that the commercial product is generally better than anything you can produce. I encourage you to seek out the best syrups you can find, because these will make all the difference in your cocktails. Two brands to try are Liquid Planet and Bigallet from France.

There are many excellent syrups produced by Torani that are useful. Just avoid their sugar-free syrups. The idea of mixing fine liquor with artificial sweeteners is ridiculous. In my opinion Torani's product line is preferred over most of Monin's line. One exception is Monin's *Curaçao Triple Sec* syrup, which is both delicious and extremely useful.

MIXOLOGY PRIOR TO 1930

One of the best collection of 19th and early 20th century recipes ever published for homemade liquors and related bar products was part of the book, *Giggle Water* by Charles Warnock (1928). This is a very rare book today. It was privately published by the author personally, and had limited distribution even at that time. Some of the more

interesting recipes from this era have been included in *Appendix C* at the back of this book (starts on page 243). This provides some insight as to just how involved the science of mixology had became during Prohibition. After the Stock Market crash, the Great Depression, and World War II, most of this science was in the category of forgotten alchemy.

Note that you should *not* attempt to make those recipes. Some contain ingredients that are now known to be toxic and/or carcinogenic. I have included this so that you can better appreciate the sophistication of cocktails back in that day when a mixologist had more in common with a chemist.

₭ LIQUOR ℒ

While the most important aspect of any cocktail, very few bartenders today have a solid understanding of how different spirits influence each other when mixed. This is why so many now prefer to blend vodka with flavoring agents, since vodka is neutral in character. Everything blends with vodka, but the same could be said of water. Most of the recipes in this book mix different base liquors together, such as rum, cognac, gin and vodka. **I have intentionally overemphasized this type of cocktail throughout this book, because it is an important tool, and one that has never been explicitly addressed.** Take the classic Long Island Iced Tea, which contains gin, rum, tequila and vodka. Why does that drink work so well, when the common wisdom today is not to mix base liquors together?

In French cooking, the combination of two parts of onion to one part each of celery and carrot is such an important flavor base that it has a special name, *mirepoix*. In Cajun cooking, a similar combination of onion, green bell pepper and celery is known as the *trinity*, and forms the underlying savory basis of countless dishes. Each flavor plays a role in the background flavor of the dish. This is the same principle at work in some of the best tropical drinks. Only instead of onion, carrot and celery, we have rum, gin and brandy. Each plays a role in the balance of the drink, but the other flavoring components such as juices, syrups, and liqueurs, are the melody. All highballs, and many tropical drinks contain less than half liquor, so spirits are not evenly matched against a bulk mixture of sugar, citric acid, and concentrated flavorings that are all competing for center stage. That is not to say that cheap and poorly manufactured spirits will suffice, because those bring foul and unpleasant tastes to the party. Inferior liquors have odd tastes that can sink any recipe. It is an irony that the finest spirits will be content to play in the background, while bargain booze will often be the only thing you can taste if you try to use it.

What I want to emphasize here is that a mixture of base liquors will make for a much more interesting and complex background harmony than simple vodka will. If you want simplicity, and to taste only the sugar and fruit, then vodka is your best choice. Such one dimensional drinks are great if you are trying to show off how you finally learned to make your own mango syrup. When the novelty of that has worn off, and you are comfortable letting your labor-intensive syrups and custom citrus-infused liquors finally mix with each other, you are ready to craft three dimensional drinks.

One starting point for a blend of base liquors for tropical drinks is two parts of rum to one part of gin. Add a bit more complexity with a little cognac. This is just a starting point, of course. You will have to experiment a lot to find what you like best, and every drink is different. Some general—and highly simplified—rules for mixing spirits when designing a new cocktail are summarized in the following Table:

Light Rum	Fire and bite. Increases the perception of alcohol.
Dark Rum	Caramel, orange and warmth. Heavy. Adds some sweetness.
Gin	Complexity and dryness. Plays especially well with liqueurs.
Brandy/Cognac	Richness and depth. Helps to mask an excessive syrup taste.
Vodka	Neutral spirit. Dilutes flavors but maintains alcohol level.
Tequila	Quite smokey and somewhat acrid. Plays well with cognac but generally not much else.
Liqueurs	Sweetness and specific flavors. Think of this as the melody.

I realize that I run the risk of meeting with harsh criticism for daring to condense an entire category of spirits into a single paragraph. This is akin to condensing all of morality down to, "Do unto others as you would have them do unto you." It is a working starting point, and you have to begin somewhere. Time and experience will enable you to expand on these ideas. **The point here is not to regard each base liquor as something that you merely flavor and call a *cocktail*. Base liquors themselves are flavors, and that can be exploited to create complexity and depth.**

ℬ BALANCE ∞

As an example of how these sample rules come into play, try mixing up the following drink. First use the proportions stated, then vary them slightly and see how the taste changes.

<u>Baseline</u>

This is an intentionally simple drink to highlight the effect of mixing together the three most common base liquors.

10 ml.	Dark Rum
10 ml.	Light Rum
20 ml.	Gin, London Dry
20 ml.	Cognac
20 ml.	Lemon juice, fresh
1 teaspoon	Grapefruit juice, fresh
15 ml.	Natural Brown Sugar Syrup (page 53)

Combine all ingredients and shake with ice. Strain into a chilled martini glass.

This drink is mathematically balanced, but it lacks a certain finesse when it comes to taste. This is what I would call a very simple two-dimensional cocktail. It is more complex in taste than its one-dimensional archetypal sibling, the Martini, but it still lacks sophistication. The following is more representative of a two-dimensional cocktail...

<u>Balancing Act</u>

Not only is this a learning experience in seeing how different liquors will smoothly fuse together, but the recipe itself is very drinkable. Taste this carefully while examining the recipe along with the Table on page 112.

10 ml.	Dark Rum
25 ml.	Light Rum
20 ml.	Gin
30 ml.	Vodka
1 teaspoon	Cognac
20 ml.	Lemon juice, fresh
30 ml.	Pineapple juice
15 ml.	Natural Brown Sugar Syrup (page 53)
4-5 drops	Angostura bitters

Combine all ingredients and shake with ice. Add a cherry if you like. Serve on the rocks with a straw.

My only real fault with this drink is that it is perhaps *too* well balanced. The character of a cocktail comes from a controlled departure from its balance. The key here is that it is a controlled departure. Balance is a starting point, but some eccentricity adds interest.

☣ ECCENTRICITY ☦

<u>Off Balance</u>

Compare with the Balancing Act on the preceding page. Added dark rum has taken the place of the vodka, and Grand Marnier has replaced the cognac. The Natural Brown Sugar Syrup has been reduced in quantity because of the extra sweetness in the Grand Marnier replacing the cognac.

40 ml.	Dark Rum
25 ml.	Light Rum
20 ml.	Gin
1 1/2 teaspoons	Grand Marnier
20 ml.	Lemon juice, fresh
30 ml.	Pineapple juice
10 ml.	Natural Brown Sugar Syrup (page 53)
4-5 drops	Angostura bitters

Same as before: Combine all ingredients and shake with ice. Add a cherry if you like. Serve on the rocks with a straw.

The balance has been perfectly maintained in terms of sweetness and alcohol, while the flavor is richer and deeper— just as you would expect based on the Table from page 112.

☣ 🍸 ☦

Chapter 3

The Margarita

The miraculous harmony of tequila, orange and lime has grown to become an eminent superstar of cocktails in terms of popularity. Like many celebrities though, years of being in the public limelight has taken its toll on this poor old girl. Psychiatrists would say that Margarita suffers from a serious case of multiple personality syndrome. Not only does she come in a dozen or more flavors now—coconut, Midori, strawberry, prickly pear cactus, raspberry, banana, peach, etc.—but dear Margarita also suffers from terrible amnesia. She doesn't remember who created her, or even what her own recipe's ratio is actually supposed to be. You would think that having one of the simplest recipes of any standard cocktail, the ratio of tequila to triple sec to lime juice would be tattooed on the cerebellum of every bartender in the world by now. Yet the ratio can easily range from 3:1:1 to 1:2:1. Tequila giant Jose Cuervo even advertises a ratio of 2:1:3, which I don't understand at all because that ratio performs poorly in taste tests. Still the ratio is just one problem. Sometimes Margarita seems to be hallucinating that she is on the Titanic, drowning in an ocean of ice, so frozen that she barely exists at all. At other times she is so harsh and aggressive that only the most chronic of alcoholics can stomach her presence. Alas, now poor Maggie is about to go completely psycho here, in what will undoubtedly be seen by many as a final indignity against this grand old lady. Once a delightfully simple drink of just three ingredients, is now reanimated by a mixological Dr. Frankenstein. It has not just been brought back to life, but transformed into a true monster among cocktails. Bear with me, though. There is a method to this madness. But first, a look at the classic...

◈ The Classic Margarita ◈

Margarita's bedraggled condition today is the result of abuse by chain restaurants that are motivated by the two biggest enemies of quality in cocktails: Profit and legal obligations. Just about any chain restaurant "Margarita" tastes more like packaged lemonade made from chemical grade citric acid and sugar stirred into a big glass of water. That's not surprising, since that is pretty close to what you are getting. The American public has came to accept this as what the drink is supposed to taste like.

Naturally, all restaurants and bars are in business to make a profit. They try to cut corners to increase their bottom line, and pouring less expensive liquor is one obvious method. Recently American restaurants have also had to contend with strict regulations concerning the amount of alcohol that can be legally served in a single portion, so in many states they can't be generous even if they want to be. Still, the real question is why was the Margarita singled out to be the victim of the most abuse of any cocktail in all of history? It may surprise you that there actually is a logical reason.

The Margarita has became synonymous with Mexican food to Americans. If a Mexican restaurant has a liquor license, you can be sure that they sell more Margaritas than any other cocktail. Often by a factor of more than ten to one. Here is the problem: The menu items in any Mexican restaurant are made mostly from beans, rice, and flour—all very inexpensive ingredients. Most of the meat being used is among the least expensive cuts available, because it is stewed for hours to make it tender anyway. There is no point in using filet mignon if you are going to boil it for two hours. Any food service business consultant will tell you that the overall profit margin doesn't get any better than it is for Mexican food. So that means they can afford to pour better drinks than other places, because they are making up the difference on the food, right? Wrong. Just the opposite. Today's college business graduates are taught that the profit margin on all items should be consistent as part of their business model. So, when it comes to running a steak house, the profit margin may be only 50% on entrees (for example) and the markup on wines is a similar 50% profit. The rules of the business model have been obeyed. When it is a Mexican restaurant, and the profit may be as high as 90% on food items, the management struggles to obtain a similar profit at the bar. Unfortunately, good tequila, fresh limes, and Grand Marnier cost a lot more than beans and rice do. So they use more ice, and generally substitute the lowest price tequila and triple sec that they can get away with. Over the last few decades consumers have been gradually weaned off of the original recipe. The arbitrary rules of modern corporate management have both demoralized and drowned poor old Margarita. Of course there is nothing actually wrong with the original recipe (whatever it was). The fault lies with the public's perception of what a Margarita should taste like after having been served acidulated sugar water for the last thirty years.

On the occasion when there is a complaint, the bartender will often try adding syrup to sweeten it up for the customer. This is a well known trick, since sugar is cheap and nine times out of ten the customer will go away feeling victorious. In their defense, they are mostly obliging customers by giving them what they want. I have experimented many times in supplying someone with an honest-to-goodness Margarita, and complaints of it being excessively sour and strong were frequent. Today customers generally *prefer* the watered-down, over-sweetened variety that they have grown accustomed to. The original Margarita *is* strong and sour, especially straight up. Like many of the drinks in this book, serving it on the rocks is acceptable if you want it weaker.

My recipe for the classic follows…

<u>Cadillac Margarita</u>

This is the only classic recipe that I am including in this book. I only make this exception because there is so much confusion about the proportions of ingredients that should be used. Although the choice of tequila is at your discretion, I have received more compliments using Cazadores *Reposada* in this recipe than with any other brand, including some tequilas that cost considerably more. Straight lime juice is used (not sweet and sour mix), which is an absolute requirement for a traditional Margarita, as served in Mexico.

70 ml.	Tequila, Cazadores *Reposada*
	or another fine tequila of your choosing
30 ml.	Grand Marnier
	or substitute Patrón *Citrónge*
30 ml.	Lime juice, fresh

Shake with ice and strain into a salt-rimmed glass that has been rubbed with the squeezed lime. I rub the entire inside of the glass with the lime, not just the rim. Either serve it straight up in a chilled Martini glass (my personal preference), or use a chilled Margarita glass, in which case you will include some of the ice from the shaker. Then float another:

| 10-15 ml. | Grand Marnier |

Garnish with a lime wedge.

◈ The Search for the Ultimate Margarita ◈

My expectations are usually pretty low when being served a mixed drink at most commercial establishments these days. It is not because I am jaded (although I am) but because one can not expect to find gold bricks on sale for 50% off. Although I have occasionally stubbed my toe running into a renegade barkeep who indulges customers with his personal belief in "quality over profit", *sub rosa*, this is not what I am talking about. Quality costs money. There is no way of getting around that. So the cocktails that intrigue me on menus are the ones priced several times higher than the going rate. For ten years the finest Margarita I had ever found in a restaurant was at the (now defunct) *Sonora Café* in Hollywood. The restaurant was owned by the same family that started the popular *El Cholo* chain in Los Angeles in the 1920's. Their Sonora affiliate was a more upscale version, with Southwestern influenced cuisine. One of Sonora's shining gems was their *24 Karat Margarita,* with a hefty price tag because they used ultra premium spirits to make it. The ingredients for this high roller model included Jose Cuervo's *Familia de Reserva* tequila and Grand Marnier *Cent Cinquantenaire* liqueur. If you watched them mixing one up, they appeared to be using bottled citrus, or sweet and sour mix, but this was not exactly true. One thing that they didn't advertise was that they prepared this mix themselves in the kitchen with freshly squeezed citrus juices, before each innocent looking bottle made its way up to the bar. Regular customers who were sufficiently inquisitive would learn that there was some secret going on in the kitchen with the sweet and sour mix, but that was all they were told. I got to know the executive chef there and eventually learned that their mix included citrus zests and lime oil (see page 47). So while the bartender appeared to be pouring from an ordinary bottled mix that you could buy, the reality was something else. The basic ratio of the Cadillac Margarita was followed, but because of the ultra-premium ingredients, it was extremely smooth and rich.

Sonora's *24 Karat Margarita* instantly became my benchmark that all other Margaritas failed to live up to. That was until one day in Carlsbad, California, at a place called the *Coyote Bar & Grill*. They have one of the largest collections of tequilas anywhere north of Mexico, and they offer both straight shots and Margaritas made with any one you like. This is when I first encountered an amazing elixir known as Porfidio *Añejo*. The packaging is distinctive because it has a green glass cactus blown into the inside of each bottle. If you asked any tequila expert at that time what was the finest tequila ever produced, they would almost certainly say Porfidio. It went out of production for many years, and although it is back again, it does not have the same depth of character that the original did.

I do not know if this story is true, but I was told that the demand for Porfidio skyrocketed soon after it became distributed in the United States. The price more than doubled in a short time, and the company in Mexico could not produce it as fast as it would sell out. The story goes that the company was desperate to take advantage of their bonanza of popularity and in order to fill orders, they began mixing other things into tequila in order to meet the demand. The taste suddenly changed and some people said it reminded them of turpentine. Again, I don't know if this true or not, but it was rumored that the Mexican government had to shut the company down because of an epic scale of adulteration. Just before that happened, sales had already fallen like a rock, as people discovered that the product had changed dramatically. Distributors had started to refuse to carry it, owing to the number of returns they were dealing with. Soon after that it disappeared completely. Many years went by. Eventually the company was reborn, although the product was not the same. The first batches the new Porfidio were available only in the kind of tiny bottles served on airplanes. The taste had almost nothing in common with the old Porfidio. Several more years would pass before they began to get back on track. The Porfidio made today is certainly a very fine tequila, but it falls short of the pre-corrupted version of the early 1990's. I know because I actually kept a bottle from the old days and did a side-by-side taste comparison with a more recent vintage. The original is darker both in color and smoky flavor, a bit sweeter, and quite a bit more intense. The new version is still an outstanding tequila, and well worth trying. If we are fortunate, with time it will return once again to become the unparalleled standard in tequilas. Porfidio is uncommon to find in liquor stores, but can be purchased online.

Margaritas made with the original Porfidio were like something from another world. Although the original formulation of Porfidio is probably gone forever, I have discovered an unlikely mixture of ingredients that produces results similar to that flavor. This happened as I was reminiscing with a bartender at the Coyote Bar over the marvelous intangible quality of the old Porfidio. When trying to describe the flavor, I said that it had a mesquite smoke flavor, and he countered saying that there was a taste of cognac that isn't normally found in tequilas. I said it wasn't exactly cognac, but something like that. I began thinking about this more and realized that it reminded me of a good quality armagnac, which has a stronger flavor than cognac. The reason is that armagnac is only distilled once (instead of twice, as in the case of cognac) and *VSOP* Armagnac is stored in special flavorful wood barrels for at least four years, during which time some water evaporates and the flavors concentrate. After more than two years of experiments, I finally produced a similar Margarita from readily available ingredients. This is not a cocktail for everyone, but I promise that it is unlike any other Margarita you have ever tasted…

<u>Tezcatlipoca Margarita</u>

Tezcatlipoca (tez-cat-lee-poh-ka) was the Aztek god of magic. His name literally means smoke and mirrors! This recipe depends strongly on Cuervo's *Black Medallion* tequila and a fine quality of armagnac. Liquid mesquite smoke is available in most large grocery stores.

45 ml.	Tequila, Jose Cuervo *Black Medallion*
30 ml.	Armagnac, Bas Hors d'âge / *VSOP*
35 ml.	Grand Marnier
60 ml.	Lime, fresh juice
3/4 teaspoon	Lime Zest - see directions below
10 ml.	Lemon, fresh juice
10 ml.	Orgeat syrup
4-8 drops	Liquid smoke, Mesquite

Grate the lime zest onto a fine mesh strainer, then slowly pour the lime juice over the zest. Pour *only* the lime juice over the zest. Press the zest against the mesh to express the liquid, then discard the zest. Combine the rest of the ingredients listed above, and shake with ½ cup of ice. Get the drink cold, but do not let the ice dilute the liquor any more than necessary. Strain into a chilled lime-rubbed, Hawaiian salt-rimmed glass and float:

10-15 ml.	Grand Marnier, ideally *Cuvee du Centenaire*

The ideal rim salt for this drink is Hawaiian red salt. There are several different types of this available at gourmet grocery stores, but you do *not* want one with very large crystals or flakes. Choose a grain just slightly larger than table salt. If all you can find is the large crystals, then grind some down gently with a mortar and pestle. I promise that this will be the most intense Margarita you have ever had in your life.

There is a reason for the slight addition of lemon juice. The limes traditionally used in Mexico for this drink are not exactly the same as the limes you usually see. They are more yellow in color and they have a slight lemon character to them.

Another example of mixing tequila with cognac…

<u>Noche Caliente</u> *(Warm Night)*

When viewing the list of ingredients in this drink, this seems to be a highly modified margarita, noting the tequila, lime and orange components, yet the combined result is quite different. Tequila is a challenging base spirit to create a totally new drink with. The flavor is very strong, and when there is enough that you can taste the tequila, one is nearly always reminded of either a Margarita or a Tequila Sunrise. This drink is an exception to that rule. The Mexican cone sugar will leave sandy bits of sugar in the drink. If you don't like that, you can substitute brown sugar syrup, or maple syrup. You can also use regular Kahlúa, but I prefer the *Mocha*.

45 ml.	Kahlúa *Mocha* liqueur
20 ml.	Tequila, Cazadores *Reposada*
20 ml.	Cognac, Hennessy *VSOP*
20 ml.	Orange Curaçao
1 ½ teaspoons	Crème d' Cacao (either white or dark)
45 ml.	Lime, fresh juice
15 ml.	Orange, fresh juice
1 teaspoon	Sugar, Mexican cone type
	or substitute the same amount of Maple Syrup
8 drops	Complexing Agent #3 (page 241)
4 drops	Angostura bitters

Shake with ice, strain into chilled glass and float an additional:

| 1 teaspoon | Tequila, ideally a fine Añejo |

Señior Chihuahua

Note that this drink is pink in color, but not to be confused with the *Pink Chihuahua* cocktail, which is simply tequila with grapefruit and cranberry juices. This is not named for the dog breed, but rather because it was discovered in Chihuahua, Mexico, far outside of the tourist area. The blend here of tequila and cognac is to better simulate the local tequila they were using. As I mentioned earlier in this book, I prefer to make my own vanilla extract for use at the bar by storing vanilla beans in a jar with just enough vodka to cover them. Be sure to slice and scrape the pods, to mix all of the pulp in with the vodka. This should be stored for at least a month before you use it, and shake it up every few days to make sure it reaches its full flavor potential. The vanilla extract produced in this manner has a very natural flavor and full flavor in cocktails.

30 ml.	Tequila, Cazadores *Reposada*
15 ml.	Cognac
45 ml.	Peach Juice
	or substitute Marie Brizard *Peche du Verger* (better)
30 ml.	Apple Juice
30 ml.	Lime Juice, fresh
1 teaspoon	Pomegranate Syrup (page 79)
	or substitute Grenadine
2-3 drops	Vanilla Extract, pure - see note above

Combine ingredients with more ice than usual and shake a bit longer. Serve it in a chilled tall (chimney) glass along with the ice. Garnish with a sprig of mint. This should always be served very cold, and is best enjoyed on a patio or beach outdoors on a hot day.

Rocko's World

The mixing of gin and tequila is fairly unusual, but not unheard of. The tequila is forced into the background here because it is overwhelmed from drowning in gin and spices. The flavor is reminiscent of Orangina, a Spanish beverage that dates back to the 1930's. The amount of curry powder in this recipe is ambiguous because it will depend on both the brand you select, and your own personal preferences. You will have to experiment some. If there isn't enough, then add more. If you put too much, drink it yourself as punishment.

50 ml.	Gin, London Dry
10 ml.	Tequila, Jose Cuervo *Especial*
25 ml.	Orange juice, fresh
25 ml.	Lime juice, fresh
1 teaspoon	Monin *Triple Sec Curaçao* syrup
sprinkle	Curry Powder - see note above

Combine all ingredients and stir with ice (do not shake). Strain into a chilled martini glass. I sometimes use a novelty garnish which is a plastic model of the Earth with a toothpick through it, as though it was a Martini olive.

As an alternative, try serving this in a Collins glass with ice, and top it with sparkling Orangina as a great hot weather refreshment.

Fire-Ita *(also known as Fire-Eater Margarita)*

If you really love hot spicy food, you just might have encountered Crazy Ed's "Satisfied Frog" *Cave Creek Chili Beer*, which contains a whole jalapeño chili pepper in every bottle. It is a good litmus test for someone who says they like spicy food. Even more tasty is a rare chili beer sold only at a couple of locations in the Grand Canyon. Although they do not have an actual chili pepper in the bottle the way that Crazy Ed's does, the flavor is delicious—and hot! If this is your kind of drink, then you will love this cocktail. The Margarita meets the chili beer. If you are a real chili-head, you'll wonder why someone didn't think of this sooner. You can substitute another tequila, but the result will not have the same jaw-dropping intensity.

40 ml.	Tequila, 1800 *Silver Reserve 100 proof*
25 ml.	Grand Marnier
25 ml.	Orange juice, fresh
15 ml.	Lemon juice, fresh
10 ml.	Lime juice, fresh
10 ml.	Monin *Triple Sec Curaçao* syrup
1/2 teaspoon	Tabasco Sauce

Combine all ingredients and shake with ice. Strain into a Margarita glass with a salt coated rim.

Chapter 4

The Scorpion

"Rediscovering this Masterpiece of Mixology"

The *Scorpion* is actually part of a family of classic tropical cocktails which figure prominently among the recipes in this book. I define this category as any sweet and sour type of cocktail that contains cognac with rum and/or gin, and some kind of almond flavor (Orgeat syrup, Noyaux, or Amaretto). Two of Trader Vic's most popular drinks for decades have been the Scorpion and the Fog Cutter. If you compare their recipes, you see that they are nearly identical. Due to copyright restrictions I can not reprint those recipes here, so just consult an old Trader Vic cocktail book and you will see what I mean. The primary difference is the float of sherry that caps the Fog Cutter, as opposed to the float of almond extract that caps Trader Vic's Scorpion. The reality is that there are some other differences that are not printed when it comes to what is actually served at the restaurant chain, but both drinks still fit perfectly into the same category—even though few patrons would realize it from the taste alone.

Just about every cocktail bar with *any* tropical drinks has something that they call a "Scorpion" on the menu, and practically no two are alike. Just as almost every bar book has a recipe for a drink by the same name, with only some vague similarity. The Scorpion originated in Hawaii, and was closely copied by Trader Vic in his early days. The recipe for the original is frequently debated. What is very likely is that some of the ingredients in the original Scorpion are no longer made, as is often the problem when trying to recreate authentic recipes that are decades old.

The challenge was to recreate the incredible original Scorpion as served in Trader Vic's first restaurant, such as it was back when Victor himself was still there. Like many others, I began by making the drink at home according to Trader Vic's own cocktail book recipe. It was only a pale shadow of the real thing. On several occasions I had the opportunity to query Vic directly about the secret going on. He never divulged anything very specific, but he did get me going on the right track with his talk of Martinique rum and that this was *more of a gin drink than people realized*. There was still more going on than that, but at least I had a starting point. That particular restaurant is gone, and the other locations don't make the drink the same way these days.

The following recipe happens to be my personal favorite cocktail. Before you scan down this list of a dozen ingredients and dismiss it as absurd, I must tell you that this recipe was honed over a period of nearly thirty years and thousands of experiments with side-by-side comparisons. It is crafted to suit my own taste, but virtually everyone that I have ever served this to has enthusiastically asked for it again.

<u>Ultimate Scorpion Tiki Bowl</u>

The gardenia flower garnish is not mandatory, but you should try your best to include it. We grow our own gardenias specifically for making this cocktail. They are a difficult plant to care for if you do not live in a tropical environment, but this one drink makes all of the effort worthwhile.

60 ml.	Gin, Hendricks
45 ml.	Cognac, Hennessy *VSOP*
30 ml.	Rum, La Favorite *Rhum Agricole Vieux*
	This is by far the best Martinique rum for this recipe
15 ml.	Orange Curaçao, DeKuyper
1 teaspoon	Crème de Noyaux
1 teaspoon	Hpnotiq liqueur
60 ml.	Lemon juice, fresh
30 ml.	Pineapple juice
1 teaspoon	Orange juice, fresh (preferably Mandarin)
20 ml.	Orange-Almond syrup (page 94)
	or substitute Trader Vic's Orgeat Syrup
1 teaspoon	Sugar Cane Syrup, ideally Martinique
4-5 drops	Grapefruit Bitters, Fee Bros.

Combine the above ingredients and shake with ice. Strain

into a chilled glass, or decorative bowl, and float on top:

2-3 drops	Almond Extract ("Pure Almond" - not synthetic)
1 each	Gardenia flower, fresh

At first I wondered why the Scorpion Tiki Bowl was only available for two or four person size portions, and then it became apparent. The number of ingredients winds up making a large volume. To reduce the proportions is not really possible, since we are already at a scale of only a few drops of some of the components. Also, it contains over five ounces of liquor, which in many states is actually illegal to serve in a single drink to someone. Thus, saying the drink is for two or more people, circumvents the legal limitation of the amount of alcohol that can be contained.

<u>Scorpion Pinch</u>

The Scorpion is the most addictive drink I know (when made properly). The combined flavor is simply remarkable. Unfortunately the chance of finding a restaurant or bar that can prepare the correct and full recipe (see above) is basically zero. During numerous business trips I found myself longing for this cocktail, and set out to improvise something that the average hotel bartender could assemble from ingredients that they would be reasonably certain to have on hand. It is pale in comparison to the real thing, but in a pinch (thus the name) it will help scratch the itch you may have. I have supplied this one recipe with ounces, since very few American bartenders are using milliliters at this time.

1 oz / 30 ml	Amaretto Disaronno
1 oz / 30 ml	Gin
³/₄ oz / 20 ml	Cognac
¹/₂ oz / 15 ml	Dark Rum
¹/₂ oz / 15 ml	Triple Sec
	or substitute Grand Marnier (better)
1 ¹/₂ oz / 45 ml	Lemon juice, fresh
1 oz / 30 ml	Pineapple juice
1 ¹/₂ teaspoons	Simple Syrup
	or substitute sugar

Combine all ingredients and shake with ice. Serve in a chilled glass with some of the ice from the shaker, and a straw.

Although Amaretto is actually herbal and does not contain any almonds (much to the surprise of most people) the flavor is never the less that of almonds. The *Scorpion Pinch* (above) substitutes Amaretto for the almond component of Orgeat, which is perfectly valid in the Scorpion family. You will see the same thing in the following recipe…

Calypso Sunset

This is a good example of how the Scorpion family is chameleon-like in character. As defined in the first part of this chapter, this drink qualifies as part of the Scorpion group, but the result is quite different in flavor. The Rum X is a pivotal player here, even though it is less than 15% of the total volume. If you doubt that, then make the same drink using ordinary rum in its place, and see for yourself.

40 ml.	Jamaican Rum, Appleton *Special*
15 ml.	Rum X (page 60)
	or substitute a fine aged rum
10 ml.	Apricot Cognac (page 69)
15 ml.	Amaretto Disaronno
25 ml.	Orange juice, fresh
15 ml.	Lemon juice, fresh
$^1/_2$ teaspoon	Pomegranate Syrup - homemade (page 79)
	or substitute Grenadine (not quite as good)

Combine all ingredients except the pomegranate syrup and shake *gently* with ice. Do not shake vigorously. Strain into a chilled martini glass. Drip in the pomegranate syrup so that it sinks to the bottom and then stir gently upwards one time to swirl the color slightly.

The similarity between the Scorpion and the Fog Cutter were mentioned at the start of this chapter. This was by design, because they wanted both of these featured drinks to compliment the food being served in the restaurant. The following drink is related to that latter classic…

<u>Fog Blaster</u>

Use the best quality dark rum you can here, as this recipe is still from the era where the rum itself was the star.

40 ml.	Dark Rum, fine quality - see note above
10 ml.	Cognac, Otard *VSOP*
15 ml.	Cointreau
1 teaspoon	Amaretto Disaronno
30 ml.	Orange juice, fresh
10 ml.	Lemon juice, fresh
3/4 teaspoon	Maple Syrup

Combine all ingredients. Shake with ice and pour into a highball glass with the ice cubes along, and add a straw. Float on top:

3/4 teaspoon	Sherry, rich (*e.g.* Lustau *East India Solara*)

If you have a quiet night, make up both a Fog Cutter and a Fog Blaster, and compare the two at your leisure. Curiously, the actual amount of alcohol in the Fog Blaster is less than the Fog Cutter, but the impression you get from drinking them is just the opposite. When put side by side, the Fog Cutter seems pretty tame, even though Trader Vic declared it to be too strong for his own personal taste. He also said the same thing about Don the Beachcomber's *Zombie*, by the way.

The following is also deserving of attention…

<u>Catalina Fog</u>

One more drink from this same versatile and flavorful family, and a personal favorite. Catalina Island is a resort destination located just off the shores of Los Angeles, and home to an entire community of millionaire yachtsmen. The apricot cognac is a matter of taste and mood. Half the time I prefer it without this ingredient, so I marked it as optional.

35 ml.	Jamaican Rum, Appleton *V/X*
15 ml.	Gin, London dry
10 ml.	Amaretto, Disaronno
10 ml.	Sherry, rich (*e.g.* Lustau *East India Solara*)
{³/4 teaspoon	Apricot Cognac (page 69) - optional}
15 ml.	Lemon juice, fresh
³/4 teaspoon	Pomegranate Syrup (page 79) or substitute Grenadine

Combine all ingredients and shake with ice. This may be served either straight up in a martini glass, or on the rocks if desired.

Chapter 5

The Matrix Concept

"A Great Bartender Can Produce Drinks That No One Else Can"

When you think about it, mixers fall into three categories; aromatic wines, fruit juices (mostly citrus), and soft drinks. One of the lesser known tricks of the trade is premixed ingredients that are simply added to spirits to create an instant cocktail with greater complexity and depth. The following is an example that can be prepared well ahead of time…

<u>Matrix</u>

3 parts	Brandy
3 parts	Lemon, fresh juice - SUPERCHARGED (page 48)
2 parts	Cherry Heering (liqueur)
	or substitute Marie Brizard's Cherry Brandy (liqueur)
2 parts	Cointreau
2 parts	Sweet Vermouth, Martini *Rosso*

This is mixed and kept cold in the refrigerator. It is used as though it were a single ingredient called, *Matrix*.

There are many possibilities with this versatile blend. One

141

example is an elegant version of the old *Tailspin* cocktail from mixing Matrix with gin and Green Chartreuse. Also be sure to try the following cocktails:

<u>Matrix Martini</u>

This is actually a half breed version of the old *Red Gin Martini*. A Red Gin Martini combines gin and a small amount of Cherry Heering. Our example of a Matrix here also contains Cherry Heering, so there is some common ground.

25 ml.	Matrix
100 ml.	Gin, Tanqueray *Ten*
2-3 drops	Angostura Bitters

Garnish with a stuffed olive or two. Personally I use an anchovy-flavored Spanish queen olive that has been hand stuffed with a piece of *Grana Padano* cheese.

<u>Matrix Carnivàle</u>

Cachaça is often described as a type of rum from Brazil. This is a mistake, though. Technically speaking, cachaça is a brandy. It is more of a commercially produced moonshine, really. The first distinction is that rum is made from molasses, while cachaça is made from raw sugar itself. In blind tastings, the flavor is perceived as "brighter and cleaner" than light rum by some, but as "less complex and less developed" by other tasters. There are many fine artisanal producers, and the key to this drink's success is in choosing a cachaça that is smooth and flavorful. Some cachaças have an unpleasant taste in this drink, so you will need to do some experimenting. The most popular cachaça drink is caipirinha—being cachaça, lime juice and sugar. This is sometimes referred to as the national cocktail of Brazil. That was the jumping off point for this cocktail. Also note that it was often the style around 1930 to have some small bits of grainy sugar in certain cocktails. The was part of the character of the drink, and to be enjoyed. If you want more of this effect, add the sugar to the glass before you pour from the shaker. If you want to make the sugar-grain effect minimal, then add the sugar to the shaker first first and swirl it around well before adding the ice cubes.

30 ml.	Matrix
50 ml.	Cachaça
1 teaspoon	Kahlúa liqueur
1 teaspoon	Lime juice, fresh
3/4 teaspoon	Maple Syrup
1/4 teaspoon	Dark Brown Sugar - see note above

Shake with ice cubes and pour into a chilled glass with some of the ice and a straw, or serve straight up as a martini style drink, if you prefer. Ideally garnish this with fresh kiwi, pineapple, and orange slices threaded on a skewer with a maraschino cherry.

<u>Matrix Islander</u>

This is a good example of the power of the Matrix concept. These few ingredients create an intensely coconut flavored drink with depth and character that seems at first simple on the palate, yet defies imitation. This is the only blended ice drink in this book. As a footnote, this is based on a unique creation once served to me at the Playboy Mansion in Los Angeles. Beware of brain freeze.

20 ml.	Matrix
40 ml.	Coconut Rum
20 ml.	Lemon Juice, fresh
1 teaspoon	Pomegranate Syrup, homemade (page 79)
1 teaspoon	Coconut Syrup (page 82)
2	Ice Cubes, standard size

Combine above ingredients in a blender. Let the blender run for about 30 seconds until well combined and frothy. Serve in a chilled small martini glass. Garnish with freshly grated nutmeg.

<u>Matrix Cuba</u>

When making this drink, do not substitute light or Jamaican rum for the dark Cuban rum, or the drink will lose most of its impact and character. My choice for this is Ron Varadera's *15 year* dark rum (there is a photo of this on page 232). You can also substitute Matusalem's 15 year Cuban style rum with acceptable results.

30 ml.	Matrix
75 ml.	Rum, dark Cuban - see note above
15 ml.	Pineapple juice
15 ml.	Lime Juice, fresh
15 ml.	Orgeat Syrup
3-5 drops	Angostura bitters

Shake with ice and strain into a chilled glass. One novelty garnish that suits this drink is a candied walnut on a stick.

To prepare the walnuts: Caramalize some sugar at 250°F. An infrared thermometer is the ideal tool for this. Then toss walnut halves in the molten sugar. Pour them out onto a silicone mat, or silicone-coated parchment paper to let them cool. While they are starting to cool, but still wet and sticky, press a wooden skewer against each one to facilitate its use. When it is completely cool, thread a maraschino cherry onto the skewer, too. The cold drink will not dissolve the sugar that attaches the walnut. The candy walnut-on-a-stick can be used to stir the drink until the person is ready to bite it off. This cocktail also works fine with a simple maraschino cherry garnish, if you want to save time.

<u>Matrix Green Peach</u>

Here is a drink that is a real crowd pleaser. I served hundreds of these at television and film parties in Hollywood during the late 1990's.

30 ml.	Matrix
50 ml.	Vodka
45 ml.	*Peche du Verger* Liqueur, Marie Brizard
	or substitute Peachtree Schnapps
15 ml.	Lime Juice, fresh

Shake with ice and serve in a chilled martini glass with a lime wedge as a garnish.

These drinks are only examples. The principle is that you prepare a complex mixture, then add a minimal number of components to create your own signature drinks that are both complex and virtually impossible to reproduce without knowing the secret basis.

ଓ   FURTHER SOPHISTICATION   ଔ

This Matrix has been simplified to make it more accessible to the reader. It could contain a great many other ingredients. Your goal is to create a very complicated flavor that will play a background chord in otherwise simple cocktails, to easily produce a signature flavor that is virtually impossible to duplicate without someone knowing the secret. In fact when I actually make up a Matrix, I usually thrown it some other exotic components in small amounts, such as dried bayberries and crystallized ginger. The more complicated you make it, the more interesting the resulting cocktail will be. Just be sure to test the mixture in a cocktail or two before you start using it, in case your personal touches went too far.

Chapter 6

Cocktails from the South Pacific

"The Birth of the Modern Cocktail"

Between the 1930's and 1940's, my father established and operated several bars in the South Pacific out of makeshift buildings and the kind of bamboo huts that Tiki bars tried to mimic. Most of these places were set up quickly and then vacated promptly as the supply of liquor ran out, or sometimes because the war was interfereing with operations. The longest lasting of these bars was the bluntly named, *Liquor - No Weather*, situated in an abandoned weather station shack in the Philippines. These fly-by-night clubs were a moment of tranquility in a sea of terror. For more about this history, refer to the first chapter of this book.

Recipes were mixed up in large quantities and stored in gallon jugs. If you only have one bartender for every hundred customers who are anxiously trying to get drunk, you have to figure out some ways to cut down the time it takes to make each drink. Everything was premixed, and the selection was limited to what was on hand at the moment. A chalkboard behind the bar listed the complete menu, which was often only three or four choices. Curiously, some of these drinks actually taste better after they have been mixed and then left to stand for a while. Try it and see for yourself.

Johnny Easter's stories about mixing up huge quantities of cocktails ahead of time were probably the inspiration for some of Trader Vic's later menu artwork. The recipes in this chapter have been scaled down to single servings. Some of the recipes have been reworked to make it possible to create the  closest flavor possible using ingredients that are currently available. The brand name of liquor I have called for here is the one that I found to produce the best result according to my own taste. Also, you will notice that there is a good deal of similarity between recipes. Not just because they were created by the same people, but also because they had to make use of the ingredients that were available.

White wine was often included in these recipes because it helped stretch the hard liquor, which was always in short supply. That is not to say that wine subtracted from quality of the drink in any way, as you will discover when you try them for yourself.

Finally, most of these drinks did not have a name in my father's notes. Most were assigned only numbers. I have given them names here based on the history of each drink.

Alongapoo Punch

This was originally prepared and served out of a punch bowl. The difference is that it contained slices of orange peel, and it was allowed to steep for several hours before it was iced down for service. At that point some fresh pineapple would be added. I have accelerated this process by using orange zest. This cocktail was the first drink that my father mixed up by the barrel and sold by the glass. It has been scaled down here for single servings, which is why many of the ingredients are in small portions here. Monin's *Amaretto Syrup* is preferable to orgeat here. I am not generally a fan of punches, but this one is really a winner.

35 ml.	Light Rum
1 teaspoon	Dark Rum
1 teaspoon	Brandy (or Cognac)
¹/₂ teaspoon	Orange Zest - see directions below
30 ml.	White Wine, dry (*e.g.* New Zealand Chardonnay)
20 ml.	Pineapple juice, ideally fresh
10 ml.	Grapefruit juice, fresh
1 teaspoon	Pomegranate Syrup, homemade (page 79)
1 teaspoon	Monin *Amaretto Syrup*
	or substitute Orgeat Syrup

| 2 pieces | Ginger Root, thin slices |
| 1 piece | Pineapple, fresh - see directions below |

Put the orange zest into a fine mesh sieve and pour the rums and brandy over it. Squeeze the zest against the sieve to press out as much of the liquid as possible, then discard the zest. Combine with the rest of the ingredients in a glass, and stir with ice. Serve in a chilled small punch glass, straining off the ginger pieces. Add a couple of ice cubes and a wedge of fresh pineapple, just as you might dip from a punch bowl.

The Tropics

Later served at the club of the same name. This one really sings of the era. As is often the case, simply reading the list of ingredients would not suggest how perfect this balance really is.

40 ml.	Rum Z (page 63)
	or substitute a smooth dark rum of your choice
20 ml.	Rum, light (preferably Cuban)
15 ml.	Lime juice, fresh
15 ml.	Pineapple juice, ideally fresh
10 ml.	Pomegranate Syrup, homemade (page 79)
1-2 drops	Angostura bitters

Shake with ice and serve on the rocks in a chilled glass. Garnish with a fresh pineapple slice.

<u>Manuia</u>

The name of this drink means "Cheers!" in the native languages of both Tahiti and Tonga. In case you were wondering, the egg white would be added fresh as the rest of the pre-mixed drink was poured into the shaker. It is hard to imagine a drink that would go better with roasted pig at a luau than this one. Consider this as a first choice to serve to someone who wants an authentic tropical drink, but doesn't care much for coconut. It is refreshing, yet still has a kick.

25 ml.	Gin, London dry
15 ml.	Brandy (or Cognac)
15 ml.	Grand Marnier originally Triple Sec, but better with Grand Marnier
15 ml.	White Wine, dry
15 ml.	Pineapple Juice
15 ml.	Orange Juice, fresh
1 teaspoon	Starfruit Syrup (page 101)
$^1/_2$	Egg White (*i.e.* half of the white of an egg)

Shake well with ice and serve in a chilled highball glass, or decorative ceramic cup. Be sure to pour everything out of the shaker to give the drink its frothy head from the egg white.

<u>Queen Salote</u>

The name of this drink is for the Queen Salote of Tonga, for whom this drink was created for back in the 1940's. The details of this occasion are described in the first chapter of this book. It is unique, having the seemingly contradictory qualities of both dry and sweet at the same time. Combining yellow persimmon syrup with gin must be done judiciously, because they multiply the astringent character of each other. Here they work in harmony, and the overall effect is truly a masterpiece for its many layers of flavors. This drink can be made without the yellow persimmon syrup, but it will lack the depth and complexity.

65 ml.	Gin, London dry
20 ml.	Orange juice, fresh
$1/4$ teaspoon	Orange Zest - see directions below
1 teaspoon	Dark Rum
10 ml.	Apricot Cognac (page 69)
2 teaspoons	Guava Paste (page 97)
20 ml.	Pineapple juice
1 teaspoon	Yellow Persimmon Syrup (page 95)
1 teaspoon	Maple Syrup
$1/4$ teaspoon	Coconut Rum - see directions below

Grate the orange zest into a fine mesh sieve and pour over the orange juice and then the gin. Press the zest to extract as much liquid as possible, then discard the zest. Add the rest of the ingredients except the coconut rum, and shake with ice. Strain off ice. Serve with a fresh orchid as a garnish. It should be noted that this drink was originally served in a coconut, which adds a slight coconut flavor and aroma. The few drops of coconut rum floated on top is intended as a substitute if you are serving this in an ordinary glass. Just be careful not to overwhelm the drink with too much coconut. The predominant flavors must remain gin, orange, guava and pineapple, coupled with the tannic dryness of the yellow persimmon syrup. This is a complicated drink with ten ingredients, so be sure not to omit anything accidentally.

Martin Johnson

This is another drink using the guava paste described in the first part of this book. The cocktail's namesake the renowned explorer, Martin Johnson, who died in a plane crash in 1937. His young wife, Osa, survived the crash and went on to chronicle her decade of safari adventures with her former husband in many books, including the best seller, *I Married Adventure* (1940). Both my father and Osa were from Kansas, and they shared a common bond, having both been explorers at a time when so many exotic parts of the world were seldom seen by Westerners.

30 ml.	Light Rum, ideally Cuban
20 ml.	Rum Z (page 63)
	or substitute a quality smooth dark rum
20 ml.	Gin, London dry
15 ml.	Lemon juice, fresh
1 1/2 teaspoons	Guava Paste (page 97)
1 teaspoon	Passion Fruit Syrup
2-3 pieces	Pineapple, preferably fresh

Bruise and lightly crush the pineapple pieces in the bottom of a cocktail shaker with a muddler. Add the rest of the ingredients and shake with ice. Strain into a chilled highball glass, discarding the pineapple pulp and ice from the shaker. Add fresh ice to the serving glass and a straw. Garnish with a fresh slice of pineapple.

<u>Blonde Buddha</u>

This was named after a local character in the Philippine Islands who ran away from Japan during the war. Although Korean by birth, she bleached her hair blonde to help make herself less Japanese looking as a precaution. Her nickname became the Blonde Buddha. That may sound racist these days, but it was actually her own idea. Eventually she stowed away on a Merchant Marine ship with the aid of the crew, and married one of the sailors when they reached port back in the United States right at the end of the war.

45 ml.	Barbados Rum, ideally Doorly's *XO*
30 ml.	Gin, Beefeater - doctored (page 65)
15 ml.	Peachtree Schnapps
15 ml.	Lime juice, fresh
1 teaspoon	Orange juice, fresh
1 teaspoon	Yellow Persimmon Syrup (page 95)
2-3 drops	Angostura bitters

Shake all ingredients with ice and strain into a chilled martini glass with an orange slice. Top with a splash of 7-Up soda.

<u>Legaspi</u>

Simple but delicious. The novel flavors of the homemade apricot cognac and starfruit syrup make this unique.

65 ml.	Gin, London dry
10 ml.	Apricot Cognac (page 69)
20 ml.	Lime juice, fresh
10 ml.	Pineapple juice
15 ml.	Starfruit Syrup (page 101)

Mix all ingredients and shake with ice cubes. Strain into a chilled tumbler along with the ice, and supply a sipping straw.

<u>Vanilla Vahine</u>

The word *vahine* simply means a young woman in Tahiti, but the word conjures images of those playful laughing sun-bronzed topless pixies that are depicted on countless Tiki bar menus. Using half a vanilla bean per cocktail may seem decadent when you are buying them at a gourmet grocery store, but they were available for pennies a pound in the islands at that time. The delicious combination of pomegranate and vanilla will confound almost anyone who did not have the advantage of reading the recipe before tasting it.

25 ml.	Rum, dark
25 ml.	Rum, light
10 ml.	Brandy or Cognac
20 ml.	Lemon juice, fresh
10 ml.	Lime juice, fresh
2 teaspoons	Pomegranate Syrup, homemade (page 79)
$^1/_2$	Egg White (*i.e.* half of the white of an egg)
$^1/_2$	Vanilla Bean, split and scraped out

Put the vanilla bean pod into the shaker with the pulp from the bean, and the other ingredients. Combine ingredients and shake vigorously with ice. Pour the frothy mixture into a chilled highball glass (including the ice) and garnish with the half vanilla bean from the recipe, and a fresh orchid.

Tahitian Dream

A dessert cocktail with the trinity of gin, rum and cognac, but not in the Scorpion family mentioned in the earlier chapter. This is an interesting recipe because there is no actual sour ingredient in the usual tropical sweet & sour formulation. The slight flavor from the lemon zest is the only contribution to the sour component.

30 ml.	Jamaican Rum, Appleton *Special*
20 ml.	Gin, London dry
1 teaspoon	Cognac
$^1/_4$ teaspoon	Lemon Zest - see directions below

20 ml.	Orange juice, fresh
30 ml.	Pineapple juice
15 ml.	Mango Syrup (page 103)
1 teaspoon	Cream of Coconut (page 82)
3-4 drops	Vanilla Extract
dash	Nutmeg, freshly grated

The amount of lemon zest is critical here because of the way this drink is mixed. Do *not* use too much zest or the drink will be overwhelmed with the flavor of the peel. First combine the rum, gin and cognac with the lemon zest in the shaker. Stir gently before adding the other ingredients. Shake with ice, then strain into a chilled martini glass (with the zest). Grate on a little fresh nutmeg. To liven it up further, garnish with a fresh edible flower.

<u>Ecuador Martini</u>

This is a departure from most of the other tropical style drinks here. It is only slightly sweet. Like the Armadillo cocktail described earlier in this book, this is a great aperitif before any pasta dish that is not too spicy.

65 ml.	Gin, Beefeater - doctored (page 65)
1/2 teaspoon	Campari
20 ml.	Orange juice, fresh
10 ml.	Lime juice, fresh
15 ml.	Tamarillo Syrup (page 98)

Combine all ingre dients. Stir gently with ice and decant into a chilled martini glass. Note that if you shake this drink, it will turn into a cloudy turbid mess. Garnish with a twist of orange peel threaded onto a short wooden skewer. Stirring the drink with the orange zest will gradually change the flavor profile of the drink, so it is left up to the recipient to decide how much is enough.

<u>Hot Buttered Witchdoctor</u>

"Clears Your Decks - A Cure for Any Ailment"

This is not the way a classic *Hot Buttered Rum* recipe goes, but the result is quite simply the best drink of its kind that I have ever tasted. You can substitute Bacardi 151 for the hard-to-find Gosling *Black Seal* 151 proof rum specified here, but the Gosling rum will produce an extraordinarily deep flavor. Prepared according to this recipe, it is strong enough to intoxicate even the most war-hardened sailor. You can tame it a bit by replacing the high-proof rum with more of the same dark rum, too. This is an example of a drink that was frequently made by sailors themselves as a kind of cure for the common cold. I remember my father giving this to me as a small child when I had a cold, as unthinkable as that would be today. This was the most expensive drink he offered in the 1940's, being more than twice the price of any other drink on the menu—yet it remained one of the most popular. Not only would it make you feel better, but it might just help you forget where you were. The first sip will probably knock you back against the wall, but if you manage to finish one to the bottom and you will see why this was so beloved. David Embury once wrote that it much easier to ruin a drink by making it too strong, than by making it too weak. Here is a drink that seems to be even stronger than the ingredients would suggest. It might just ruin you.

60 ml.	Dark Bermuda Rum, Gosling's *Black Seal* or substitute Barcardi *Black*
30 ml.	151 proof Rum, Gosling's *Black Seal 151*
30 ml.	White Wine, dry
15 ml.	Sherry, Dry Sack *Solera Oloroso 15 Year* or substitute another rich sherry
15 ml.	Grand Marnier
2 each	Cloves, freshly crushed
2 each	Allspice Berries, freshly crushed
pinch	Cinnamon, ground
1 strip	Orange Rind
1 teaspoon	Honey
5 drops	Complexing Agent #1 (page 240)
1 teaspoon	Butter - see directions below

Mix these ingredients in a cup and then immerse the cup (or shaker) in a pan of boiling water for a couple of minutes, being sure to dissolve the honey completely. Then pour through a strainer into a glass that has a pat of butter in it. Stir to help dissolve the butter. A swizzle stick with a curl of orange peel is the optional garnish. You may also choose to add freshly grated nutmeg, but this is not part of the original recipe. Regardless of the finishing touches, this drink is as memorable as it is powerful.

These next two recipes call for Ginseng Syrup, which was readily available in Asia at the time, being sold as a Chinese medicine for various ailments.

Nerve Tonic

Like the previous recipe, this is sort of therapeutic cocktail. It actually does seem to induce a tranquil state, interestingly. Many patent medicine *nerve tonics* were widely marketed in the early 19th through 20th centuries. Most contained vegetable extracts. Some contained nothing. Some contained 

Russian Ginseng Syrup

narcotics like opium, cocaine and heroin. Nearly all of them contained a lot of alcohol. The active ingredients in this tonic is alcohol and ginseng. Ginseng syrup tastes very good, and so it can be used to produce some novel cocktails. It is generally difficult to find in the United States. Inquire at Asian food stores, particularly Korean markets if you have one in your area. If you do find some, be sure to taste it before mixing a drink with it. The flavor should be very sweet, as other bar syrups are. If it is not sweet enough, then it may need to be diluted with simple syrup to the right concentration for use. It should taste of ginseng, but not be medicinal tasting. There is a company called *Canadian Ginseng* that sells the roots by mail (order online) and then you can prepare a syrup yourself using pieces of the root with sugar and water in the same way that other syrups were shown earlier in this book. If you are fortunate enough to travel to China, Japan, Korea, or Russia, you can purchase bottles of ginseng syrup inexpensively at many grocery stores. The pisco, maple syrup and allspice here have been used to simulate the original native liquor that is commercially unavailable.

50 ml.	Pisco
15 ml.	Rum, dark Haitian
45 ml.	Grapefruit juice, fresh
25 ml.	Lime juice, fresh
20 ml.	Ginseng Syrup - see text above
$1/2$ teaspoon	Maple Syrup
3 each	Allspice Berries, freshly crushed
splash	Tonic Water - see directions below

Combine all ingredients except tonic and shake with ice. Strain through a fine mesh sieve to remove the allspice berry fragments. Serve in a large rocks glass with some shaved ice and a splash of Tonic. A sprig of mint is a garnish is optional.

The taste is very unusual. Like nothing else—and I do not say that lightly.

<u>Lady Drink Number 1</u>

Probably inspired by the Pink Lady cocktail, but without the fresh cream that would have been hard to come by in the South Pacific during the war. This is another fine example of a brilliant balance. Reading the recipe, this probably does not strike you as being anything remarkable, but the result is both sophisticated and beguiling. See the notes on the previous cocktail regarding the Ginseng Syrup. To make this more elegant, use a fine quality of gin, but to make it authentic, use a low quality of gin! The native girls that the sailors would bring in to the bar wouldn't know the difference between good and bad gin, so they were invariably served the cheapest kind on hand. What is surprising is that this drink is remarkably good with inferior gin. I dare say that I actually prefer a lesser quality of gin in this cocktail. Try it and see for yourself.

60 ml.	Gin - see note above
15 ml.	Cherry Heering
	or substitute Marie Brizard's *Cherry Brandy* (liqueur)
30 ml.	Lemon Juice, fresh
10 ml.	Ginseng Syrup
1 teaspoon	Egg White

Shake very hard with ice and strain into a chilled martini

glass with a cherry garnish.

<u>Lezat</u>

Just as the Mai Tai got its name from a Tahitian who proclaimed it *the best* in his native tongue, *lezat* means "delicious" in Indonesian. This is quite an intriguing concoction.

40 ml.	Barbados Rum, R.L. Seales *10 Year*
20 ml.	Cointreau
25 ml.	Madeira
20 ml.	Lime juice, fresh
1 teaspoon	Natural Brown Sugar Syrup (page 53)

Combine all ingredients and shake with ice. Strain into a chilled glass. Garnish with a lime wedge, if you wish.

<u>Diamond Rose</u>

The Sour Cherry syrup used here can be found at some health food stores in the United States. Do *not* use regular cherry syrup or the drink will be far too sweet. In Europe, look for Garden brand *Cherry Fruit Syrup* made in Poland. Although it does not explicitly say "sour cherry" on the label, as American brands do, it is from sour cherries.

60 ml.	Rum X (page 60)
	or substitute light rum, or a blend of the two
20 ml.	Lime juice, fresh

10 ml.	Sour Cherry Syrup - see note above
4-6 drops	Peychaud's Bitters
35 ml.	7-up soda - see directions below

Mix rum, lime juice, cherry syrup and bitters in a shaker with ice. Pour into a chilled tumbler along with the ice. Splash on the 7-up soda on top.

French Apple Pie

Definitely in the category of a dessert drink, but far more flavorful than any *Appletini* you could ever imagine. The coconut rum and butterscotch schnapps work to recreate the flavor profile of a kind of rum that is no longer available.

45 ml.	Calvados
30 ml.	Dark Rum, Bacardi *Black*
20 ml.	Jamaican Rum, Appleton *Special*
1 teaspoon	Coconut Rum, DeKuyper *Tropical Coconut*
1 teaspoon	Butterscotch Schnapps, Hiram Walker
60 ml.	Apple juice
10 ml.	Lemon juice, fresh
10 ml.	Natural Brown Sugar Syrup (page 53)
2 pinches	Cinnamon, ground

Combine all ingredients. Shake with ice and either divide between two smaller martini glasses, or alternatively serve in a single chilled glass as a single portion, with a straw. This drink can also be served at room temperature—which was often out of necessity originally, since ice was not always readily available. Try coating the rim of the glasses with a mixture of brown sugar and cinnamon as a nice touch to make it even more of a special dessert drink, but this was not part of the original recipe.

Christmas Island Cocktail

This drink remains one of my absolute all time favorites. The taste is indescribable and exquisite. The taste relies on the Zacapa *23 Year* rum specified. I have tried many other kinds in this recipe, and no other rum came close.

30 ml.	Benedictine liqueur
25 ml.	Rum, Ron Zacapa *23 Year*
15 ml.	Apricot Brandy, Hiram Walker
10 ml.	Coconut Rum, DeKuyper *Tropical Coconut*
1 1/2 teaspoons	Cognac, Hennessy *VSOP*
30 ml.	Pineapple juice
15 ml.	Lemon juice, fresh
6-8 drops	Complexing Agent #3 (page 241)

Shake with ice and serve straight-up in a martini glass.

Captain Smith

"A couple of these and you'll feel like you hit an iceberg."

Named after the captain of the Titanic. Simpler than many of the other recipes here, this is delicious and nostalgic. You won't really understand what I mean by *nostalgic* until you try it yourself. Not what you would probably expect from just reading the recipe.

60 ml.	Jamaican Rum, Appleton *Special*
20 ml.	Dark Cuban Rum, Havana Club *7-year* or substitute Rum Z (page 63)
10 ml.	Lemon juice, fresh
10 ml.	Lime juice, fresh
10 ml.	Passion Fruit Syrup, homemade (page 100) or substitute Fee Bros. Golden Passion Fruit Syrup
10 ml.	Maple Syrup
3-5 drops	Orange bitters (not original, but suggested)

Combine all ingredients and shake with ice. Originally you pour this into a glass with a lot of ice (naturally, given the theme of the drink!) but I prefer to strain into a chilled cocktail glass. The garnish was a small toy plastic lifeboat.

Italian Pirate King

Based on the classic *Italian Pirate* cocktail. There are many versions of the original, calling for spiced rum with Campari and/or Grand Marnier. Since many spiced rums are nothing more than a low quality rum masked with sugar and artificial flavors, you are better off adding your own spices to a quality rum here. If you can not obtain actual Cuban rum, then I suggest using Ron Matusalem *Platino* and *Gran Reserva* for the light and dark rums, respectively.

50 ml.	Rum, dark Cuban
15 ml.	Rum, light Cuban
30 ml.	Apricot Brandy, Marie Brizard
15 ml.	Orange liqueur, Harlequin
	or substitute Cointreau
15 ml.	Aperol (an Italian aperitif)
1 ½ teaspoons	Chambord raspberry liqueur
30 ml.	Lemon, fresh juice
30 ml.	Lime, fresh juice
15 ml.	Orange-Almond Syrup (page 94)
pinch	Cinnamon, ground

Combine all ingredients and shake with ice. Strain into either one large, or two small glasses. This serves well in hand blown decorative amethyst or gold goblets.

Bahama Bomber

Loosely based on the original *Bahama Mama* (not to be confused with some of the bizarre concoctions that have been published online in recent years, calling for everything from cranberry juice to coffee). Note that although Marie Brizard's Coconut Liqueur is more intensely coconut flavored than other coconut rums. Nassau Royale liqueur is essential to any authentic drink in this category. Both are uncommon in liquor stores, but easily found online.

| 50 ml. | Rum, Pyrat *XO* |
| 15 ml. | Nassau Royale liqueur |

15 ml.	Coconut liqueur, Marie Brizàrd
	or a Coconut Rum (not as good)
15 ml.	Orange Curaçao
75 ml.	Pineapple juice
30 ml.	Orange juice, fresh
3-4 drops	Angostura bitters

Combine all ingredients. Shake with ice, pour into a tall glass. Then float:

10 ml.	151 proof Rum, Gosling's *Black Seal 151*
	or substitute Bacardi *151 proof Rum*
2-3 drops	Vanilla extract

Float the vanilla extract on top of the foam, then add the high-proof rum.

<u>Kiau Karamikah</u>

Headhunting natives living along the Sepik River were introduced to this drink while trading with them during the course of the war. They named this drink Kiau Karamikah, meaning "from the ocean" in their own language, because sailors had brought it to them. For more about the interesting history and events that led up to this encounter, see the first chapter in this book. The recipe has been modified here for ingredients you can obtain today. For more about Brazilian cachaça, see page 142 under *Matrix Carnivàle*.

| 30 ml. | Cachaça |

30 ml.	Rum, Jamaican, Appleton *Special*
30 ml.	Lemon juice, fresh
20 ml.	Passion Fruit Syrup, homemade (page 100)
15 ml.	Orange Curaçao
	or substitute Grand Marnier
10 ml.	Natural Brown Sugar Syrup (page 53)
4-6 drops	Complexing Agent #2 (page 240)

Combine all ingredients. Shake with ice and strain into a chilled glass. If you want to make it more authentic, then serve it at room temperature. I think it is safe to assume that there were very few martini glasses in the middle of New Guinea in the 1940's, and even fewer ice cubes. You might even consider drinking it from a canteen, if you want to recreate the original experience.

Popeye

Named after a bosun who had a peculiar medical condition that enabled him to push one eye partially out of its socket by contracting facial muscles. You can imagine how well that went over with the ladies. Try not to think about that while sipping this. Previously I have recommended Garden brand syrups (made in Poland) for their Sour Cherry and Strawberry flavors. Their Orange Syrup is *not* good in this drink. If you can't find a better fragrant and natural tasting orange syrup, your best option will be Monin *Curaçao Triple Sec* syrup.

| 30 ml. | Dark Rum, Bacardi *Black* |

30 ml.	Cognac
15 ml.	Cherry Brandy (liqueur), Marie Brizard
10 ml.	Cointreau
60 ml.	Lime juice, fresh
30 ml.	Orange juice, fresh
20 ml.	Orange Syrup - see note above
	or Monin Curaçao Triple Sec Syrup
3-4 drops	Complexing Agent #2 (page 240)

Shake with ice and strain into glass. Dust with:

| ¼ t. | Black Pepper, freshly ground (fine grind) |

The combination of flavors together with the black pepper spice is remarkably sophisticated.

ଛ Y ଌ

Chapter 7

The Modern Interpretation

"Quality is Largely the Density of the Flavor Experience"

Even though you don't consciously think about it, the *density of flavor experience* is usually the first consideration when deciding which drink to prepare for someone you just met. The spectrum ranges from light low-alcohol summer drinks served in large glasses with plenty of ice, to those intensely-flavored knee-buckling cocktails that can taste like rocket fuel going down. My personal preference leans strongly towards the latter category, as you can tell from most of the recipes in this book. In my opinion, a tall drink with a cup of ice is a waste of whatever spirit may have been drowned in it. Besides, you really don't need any skills in mixology to add a half ounce of vodka to a glass of iced tea and a wedge of lemon—and, yes, that is actually served up as a "cocktail" in two American establishments I have visited. The more diluted a cocktail is, the less need there is for balance. Almost any combination of inferior spirits can be consumed if sufficiently diluted, because the flavor is covered up by the neutrality of the water. The test of a well balanced drink is to try it straight up. If you want to dilute it down from there, that's up to you. Highly diluted cocktails used to be referred to as "beginner drinks." These days they are the norm in most establishments, because ice is cheap and every business want to make money. To the delight of bar owners everywhere, the public has finally accepted the idea that a cocktail can be mostly ice and water.

If someone can take sips of a cocktail without losing their train of thought, the drink has failed to capture their attention. The greater the *density of flavor experience*, the more there is to capture your senses and draw your focus away from everything else that might be going on in the room at that moment. My philosophy is that the longer your attention can be drawn away from every other thought, and focused only on the flavors that you alone are experiencing at that moment in time, the more successful that cocktail ranks.

THE ZOMBIE

The Zombie is credited as an invention of Don the Beachcomber in 1934, he did not publish a recipe for it until 1950. Even then the recipe was obscure, appearing only once on a page in a very rare barbecue cookbook that he published himself in a three-ring binder. Because of the popularity and lore of this macabre drink, other mixologists attempted to reverse engineer his recipe and deduce the ingredients for years. Included among those mixologists was Trader Vic, who in 1943 proclaimed that he had the recipe figured out. Only he didn't. At least not according to Don the Beachcomber. In fact none of the many recipes of the 1930's and 1940's named "Zombie" were very similar to what Don swore that the drink actually contained in his 1950 revelation. According to him, there was pineapple juice (not orange juice), passion fruit syrup (which I don't believe anyone else ever guessed), and no absinthe or anise (which nearly everyone did guess). Don swore that this 1950 recipe was absolutely genuine and, "anyone who says otherwise is a liar." Given Don's secretive nature, I still don't entirely trust his confession here.

Even the employees at Don the Beachcomber's did not know the ingredients. It was mixed from numbered bottles, and all they were told was the proportion of each bottle to pour. This was the way he guarded the secrets of all of his famous drinks. The problem here is that some of the attempts at creating a Zombie by other bars became more well known than Don's own original recipe (assuming that he was telling the truth when he divulged that recipe in 1950, of course). My own theory is that the Zombie suffered the same fate as the Mai Tai. Don was probably mixing his Zombies with ultra-premium rums initially, but as the demand for high quality rum increased over the years, it became prohibitively expensive later (see the first part of this book for more on that phenomenon). At the same time other bars were also experiencing shortages of quality rum, especially during the war years. Most people who tried to recreate Don's Zombie believed that there should be a little absinthe, or some other anise liqueur in the drink. Don said no, but it had already became what customers expected when they ordered the drink. Also note that both of the versions here make use of citrus zest, which was not part of the original recipe (or any of the other versions from that entire era, as far as I know).

During the 1990's there was a significant decline in the number and quality of tropical theme clubs. One of the few glimmers of light that came across my path was named Wokcano (an awkward hybridization of the words *wok* and *volcano*). The interior of Wokcano was a half-hearted attempt to recreate the Tiki genre, complete with bamboo huts constructed over a few of the tables, colored lighting, and a mixture of modern imported Asian and Polynesian theme decor. One of the few genuinely authentic elements was a drink menu that had vintage style drawings of the cocktails. In the early days of the establishment, the quality of some their drinks was outstanding. The original bartender is long gone, though. Back in the day, the one drink that was especially impressive was his version of the classic Zombie. Not only was it was one of the best cocktails that I'd ever had in a restaurant, but it was especially surprising because I had never been a fan of the Zombie before. Naturally I wanted to know what they were putting into it. Like Don the

Beachcomber, he also wanted to keep it a secret. He had one problem, though. It wasn't his restaurant, so he didn't have a private locked room to do his mixing in.

Most of their drinks were mixed behind the bar when they were ordered, but the Zombie was poured from a plain white plastic bottle, so there was no way of telling what was in it. This drink was prepared ahead of time in the kitchen — a sure sign that there is a secret involved. I visited the place many times and eventually convinced one of the waitresses to report back to me about exactly what was going on in the kitchen. She told me that there was a huge bottle in the back that had pieces of citrus peel and pineapple slices in the liquor, and a valve at the bottom to drain the liquid from. This is a very old method of supercharging. I've seen it used in both Italy and Mexico. Unfortunately it leads to highly variable results because there is no way to keep the balance constant. You add more spirits, and the old fruit is still in there. It contributes something, but not as much as fresh fruit does. How much additional fruit should be added? After you guess this a couple of times, you now have a range of different ages of fruit mixed together, and the different ages of fruit contribute different types of flavors. Then there's the fact that you can only add so much fruit before the bottle starts to fill up. At some point you have to dump it out and start over. At that moment the flavor changes abruptly again. I had already noticed that sometimes the drink was great, and sometimes not. Now I knew why.

The recipe I have provided below will produce the same drink every time. The other secret was the substitution of cognac for a some of the rum, which I had already guessed after the discovery I made earlier when trying to recreate the original Porfidio Margarita (see Chapter 3). I have made further improvements since that time, and now present you with the best version to date…

Volcano Zombie

Be sure to use fresh pineapple for this, and not canned. I have been told that fresh pineapple has active enzymes in it that are responsible for the transformation of this mixture during its storage (see directions below). I have some doubt as to whether or not this is true, though. Both alcohol and acid (lemon juice) denature proteins, plus most enzymes are inactive when they are cold. Still, something is definitely going on here, because the flavor changes after storage. Test this yourself by making up a fresh batch and comparing the flavor with one that has been stored 24 hours in the refrigerator. You will see the benefit of making it ahead.

60 ml.	Myer's Dark Rum, *Planter's Punch* or substitute Rum Z (page 63)
¹/₂ teaspoon	Orange Zest - see directions below
¹/₄ teaspoon	Lemon Zest - see directions below

20 ml.	Cognac
10 ml.	151 proof Rum - see notes below
1/4 teaspoon	Pernod liqueur
	or substitute Pernod Absinthe (better)
25 ml.	Lemon juice, fresh
30 ml.	Orange juice, fresh
25 ml.	Cointreau
	or substitute Grand Marnier (a bit too rich, though)
1 teaspoon	Maple Syrup
1 teaspoon	Pomegranate Syrup (page 79)
	or substitute Grenadine
2-3 pieces	Pineapple, fresh and very ripe

Grate the zest into a fine mesh sieve and pour the dark rum over it (pour *only* that rum over the zests). Press the mixture of zests against the mesh to express as much liquid as possible. Discard the zests. Then combine with the other ingredients, but no ice at all. Mix in and crush the pineapple just a little bit. Refrigerate these ingredients together for at least two hours, but overnight is better. Three days at the most. As described above, there is a positive change in flavor during the storage as it becomes mellower, and smoother, so try to resist the urge to raid the fridge before it is ripe.

Obviously you can multiply the quantity of ingredients and prepare as many drinks ahead of time as you anticipate wanting. When ready to serve, pour this through a strainer over a few ice cubes in a tall glass, and add a piece of the pineapple a skewer. Note that since no ice has actually been shaken with the drink, this has effectively made the drink stronger. Usually much more high-proof rum is added. Here we simply cut back on the ice by getting the drink cold in the refrigerator ahead of time. The taste is much better than compensating for the dilution of the ice with more alcohol. In general, this is an important technique to have in your toolbox. Storing premixed drinks in the refrigerator, and then pouring them over ice when serving increases the alcohol concentration, and reduces the problem of excessive dilution due to slow consumption. For more on the topic of dilution in drinks, see the subsection titled, "Ice" in an earlier part of this book (page 85).

Wong Jing Golden

This delicious drink is prepared in Hong Kong at a small bar, Wong Jing. It is closely related to Don the Beachcomber's original *Zombie*, and also (obviously) has some common ground with the *Volcano Zombie* described in the previous recipe. Wong Jing's is also a secret, but between the menu description and watching the bartender, the following recipe was cobbled together. This one is not stored ahead of time, and it contains more sugar in the form of more syrup and pineapple juice. Note that the 3:2:1 ratio of pineapple-lemon-orange juice is a single-bottle ingredient in Asian bars that I have seen many times now. I have even seen the acronym "P-L-O" in English letters a couple of times. In this drink use either white or green cardamom pods. Do *not* use black cardamom pods! They are very different in flavor. The white pods are actually green pods that have been bleached, which gives them a slightly different flavor. In cocktails the white type seem to generally work better. You can try this with green and see which you like, but black is definitely not an option. Black cardamom tastes something like burning sulfur and smoke in a cocktail. Also note that the exact amount of passion fruit syrup will depend on personal taste and which orange liqueur you are using.

30 ml.	Dark Rum
25 ml.	Light Rum
3/4 teaspoon	Lemon Zest - see directions below
3/4 teaspoon	Orange Zest - see directions below
30 ml.	Pineapple juice
20 ml.	Lemon juice, fresh
10 ml.	Orange juice, fresh
10-15 ml.	Passion Fruit Syrup (page 100) or Fee Bros. Golden Passion Fruit Syrup
10 ml.	Mandarine Napoleon Orange Liqueur or substitute Grand Marnier
2 each	Cardamom Pods, crushed - see note above

Put the lemon and orange zests in a fine mesh sieve and slowly pour over the two rums. Rub the zests to get as much through as possible. Discard the zests. Add the rest of the ingredients and shake with ice. Strain into a chilled glass and garnish. The garnish used at the restaurant requires a master, and even then it takes him several minutes per drink. They can afford this time, since the cocktail is extremely expensive. The garnish is impossible to copy, but you don't drink the garnish.

THE MIDORI DAIQURI

The MD was born in New York's *Studio 54* disco in 1978, when Suntory first introduced this Japanese green melon flavored liqueur to America. As with every other flavored Daiquiri of the disco era, it was to be blended with copious amounts of ice and sugar, making it more like a snow cone than a cocktail. Food historians generally believe that the original Daiquiri was invented in Cuba around 1905 by mining engineers. The drink is named after Daiquiri Beach near Santiago, Cuba, where they were working. The original Daiquiri described by these Cuban engineers was simply rum, lime juice, and sugar. I am somewhat skeptical of this story, though. Cocktails containing citrus juice, sugar and liquor go back hundreds of years. Cubans sitting around making drinks with local Cuban rum, Cuban sugar and Cuban limes seems like it should have happened long before 1905.

As I mentioned in the first part of this book, one of my favorite places in Los Angeles had been Alan Hale's *Lobster*

Barrel. It had been over a decade since I ordered a Midori Daiquiri—or anything else that was fluorescent green in color—when the *Skipper* urged me to give it a try. This was one of those moments when you realize that your preconceptions about something were based on your personal bad experiences. This was a very different MD. There was no ice, and the flavor was complex and not cloying. I knew that there was a lot more going on in this drink than just Midori, rum and lime juice. Although he never gave me the exact recipe, he dropped enough hints over time that I was able to produce an identical tasting drink eventually.

Some ten years later at *Iron Chef* Morimoto's restaurant in Philadelphia, I found another stab at the perfect Midori Daiquiri. Based on the radioactive green color, they call it the E=MC (not E=MC^2, which is either a typographical error on the menu, or Morimoto failed physics). While the E=MC is very good, it differs from Alan Hale's version. Here I have combined elements from each for the best of both.

45 ml.	Midori Melon Liqueur
15 ml.	Light Rum
15 ml.	Vodka
10 ml.	Cointreau
30 ml.	Lemon juice, fresh
15 ml.	Lime juice, fresh
10 ml.	Kiwi Syrup, Torani - see note below
$^1/_2$ teaspoon	Yuzu extract (page 84)

Shake with ice and serve in a large chilled martini glass. Note that within the United States, Torani syrups can be found online. One source is lollicupstore.com

Carlton St. Moritz

This drink was invented in the Swiss hotel of the same name, but not at their bar. Rather in a private hotel room there employing mostly items salvaged from leftovers of breakfast that had been delivered by room service (grapefruit juice, maple syrup, and Swiss cocoa) together with those little travel size bottles of liquor you get on airplanes. While the atmosphere of this beautiful Swiss resort area made the drink quite special, it still remains one of my personal favorite evening cocktails in any setting. I have served this to many guests, and it never fails to baffle them as to what the ingredients are. This is the magic of mixology is at its best; relatively simple ingredients combined to produce something that is delicious and mysterious.

60 ml.	Light Rum, Puerto Rican
30 ml.	Amaretto, Disaronno
30 ml.	Grapefruit juice, fresh
1/4 teaspoon	Cocoa Powder (99% cacao)
1 teaspoon	Maple Syrup
1 teaspoon	Egg White

Shake with ice and strain into a chilled martini glass. The

egg white was not part of the original concoction, but adds a nice froth and smoother finish.

Passion Fruit Cocktail

This is both rich and powerful. Much more than the sum of its parts.

30 ml.	Vodka, Stolichnaya *100 proof*
15 ml.	Cognac
15 ml.	Rum, light
15 ml.	Lemon juice, fresh
15 ml.	Passion Fruit Syrup, homemade (page 100)
	or substitute Fee Bros. Passion Fruit Syrup
10 ml.	Parfait Amour, Marie Brizard
	or substitute Cointreau (not as good here)
1/2 each	Passion Fruit - see directions below

Scoop out the pulp from half of a passion fruit, and put it into the shaker with the other ingredients. Shake with ice and decant into a chilled martini glass. The seeds of the passion fruit are edible.

The following drink has is on the same wavelength…

Kamehameha

Named for one of the great kings of Hawaii. This drink is an interplay of lime and passion fruit, with a subliminal background of Frangelico that beguiles the palate. The orange juice acts more as a liaison between the other dominant flavors. Being made with vodka instead of rum, this is not exactly a traditional Tiki drink, but the taste is still in the same genre. Don't bother mixing this up with rum instead, either. Like every other recipe in this book, variations and substitutions have been tried repeatedly over the years and sampled endlessly. Even though it may seem counterintuitive, vodka is absolutely the best choice here. Otard cognac has some peculiar notes that work especially well here, but other cognacs may be used with acceptable results.

40 ml.	Vodka
20 ml.	Lime juice, fresh
1/4 teaspoon	Lime Zest - see directions below
25 ml.	Cognac, Otard *VSOP*
3/4 teaspoon	Frangelico liqueur
40 ml.	Orange juice, fresh
10 ml.	Passion Fruit Syrup (page 100)
	or substitute Fee Bros. Golden Passion Fruit Syrup
10 ml.	Amaro Nonino (an Italian liqueur)

Grate the lime zest into a fine mesh strainer. Squeeze the lime juice through the zest. Then slowly pour the vodka through the same zest. Discard the zest. Combine the rest of the ingredients and shake with ice. Pour into a chilled glass with a few of the ice cubes and serve with a long straw.

<u>Gin Fusion</u>

I'm almost afraid to admit where this recipe came from, but I must give credit where credit is due. There was a restaurant in a large metropolitan airport terminal that served an array of Asian foods, including Thai, Chinese and Japanese food together on one menu. The food was mediocre, but some of the cocktails were surprisingly good. One was outstanding. This was the star drink of the establishment— and I actually ordered every single drink on the bar menu hoping to find another gem like this. This was back when there were no laws about how much you could be served.

75 ml.	Gin, Tanqueray *Number Ten*
1 teaspoon	Apricot Brandy, Hiram Walker
20 ml.	Lemon, fresh juice
20 ml.	Pineapple juice
20 ml.	Falernum syrup, Fee Bros.
1/2 teaspoon	Cilantro, freshly minced
1/2 teaspoon	Ginger, freshly minced
6-8 drops	Complexing Agent #2 (page 240)

Muddle ginger with lemon juice. Mix other ingredients together, shake with ice and strain into a chilled martini glass. Some small bits of cilantro should have made their way into the glass.

Many years (and thousands of miles) later, I came across another ginger flavored gin cocktail in an Australian bar. This one is a crowd pleaser because of the intriguing color. They were kind enough to actually supply me with the recipe for this one directly.

Aussie Blue Gin

Quoting the bartender, "It looks like a swimming pool in summer. It tastes a lot better though. No chlorine." They were using a bottled Pineapple Orange juice blend, but fresh juice is only better if you can get excellent sweet oranges. Otherwise Tropicana's blend may be your best option.

60 ml.	Gin, Beefeater - doctored (page 65)
20 ml.	Lemon Juice, fresh
20 ml.	Blue Curaçao
10 ml.	Pineapple juice
10 ml.	Orange juice, fresh
1 teaspoon	Simple Syrup
1 teaspoon	Ginger, freshly chopped up

Shake with ice and strain through a sieve into a chilled martini glass. Garnish with a spiral of orange peel.

Green Jin and Green Jinger

If you add ginger to the *Green Jin*, you have a *Green Jinger*. Both are subtle and sophisticated. Either one could be the signature cocktail of a club or restaurant. The complexing agent will ensure that guests will never be able to duplicate it themselves. Maraschino liqueur is uncommon in liquor stores these days, but it is readily available online.

50 ml.	Gin, Juniper Green Gin
30 ml.	Vodka, preferably Russian
10 ml.	Lemon juice, fresh
15 ml.	Natural Brown Sugar Syrup (page 53)
4-6 drops	Complexing Agent #1 (page 240)
1/2 teaspoon	Luxardo *Maraschino Liqueur*
1 wedge	Green Apple, chopped - see directions below
2 thin slices	Ginger, fresh (optional - see note above)

Roughly chop the apple. Muddle the apple pieces in the bottom of a shaker with the other ingredients. Add a lot of ice cubes and shake well. Strain into a chilled martini glass. Some little bits of apple will get in, but that's part of the drink.

Ten Blue

Unlike most of the cocktails in this book, here is one that is not especially strong. Notice the 3:2:1 ratio of pineapple, lemon, and orange juices, as in the previous recipe. The blueberry preserves called for in this recipe are available in most grocery stores in larger cities around the world. Do not substitute this ingredient, because these particular preserves are low in sugar and contain a great deal of blueberry fruit. Also, be sure to measure carefully (see page 43).

45 ml.	Gin, Tanqueray *Ten*

15 ml.	Blueberry Liqueur, DeKuyper
	or substitute 20 ml. Lapponia Blueberry liqueur
30 ml.	Pineapple juice,
20 ml.	Lemon juice, fresh
10 ml.	Orange juice, fresh
1 teaspoon	St. Dalfour French Blueberry Preserves

Combine all ingredients and shake well with ice cubes. Strain into an oversized chilled martini glass. I have some large six ounce cobalt blue martini glasses that I use exclusively for this drink. A long skewer threaded with sugar-glazed blueberries layed across the top of the glass makes a nice garnish for this. To prepare the blueberries, simply toss fresh berries with powdered sugar and refrigerate under plastic wrap for several hours. The sugar will draw out moisture from the berries and sweeten them at the same time.

Kat M

You might notice the similarity of this to the *Blonde Buddha* cocktail of the 1940's described in the previous chapter. This one is every bit as enchanting, but with more of an impish Vegas attitude. Evervess sodas are made in Denmark and marketed throughout Europe. In the United States it will be easier to find Schweppes.

65 ml.	Rum X (page 60)
	or substitute a quality light rum, or a blend the two
40 ml.	Gin, Beefeater - doctored (page 65)

20 ml.	Marie Brizard *Peche du Verger*
	or substitute Peachtree Schnapps (different, but good)
10 ml.	Orange juice, fresh
40 ml.	Evervess *Bitter Lemon*
	or substitute Schweppes *Original Bitter Lemon*
³/₄ teaspoon	Yellow Persimmon Syrup (page 95)

Combine all of the ingredients except the Evervess soda, and shake with ice. Strain into a chilled martini glass and then pour on the Bitter Lemon soda last.

Oro Avanti

The name is Italian for "gold is ahead." This drink was originally made with a unique native burnt coconut liquor that is not available commercially. The vinegar, sherry and allspice have been added to ordinary coconut rum in order to approximate the flavor, and I must say that the simulation is actually better than the original. The coconut flavor is almost completely invisible, which will come as a surprise. This is a peculiar drink that will confound almost anyone as to what is in it. Many people love it, and it is always fun to watch their reaction when you tell them that there is vinegar in their drink. Just be sure to use very high quality of balsamic vinegar, and *not* the typical grocery store variety. Fine balsamic vinegars are aged for 25 to 100 years, and are sometimes served straight in small glasses as an aperitif in Italy. That is the quality of balsamic vinegar *required* in this recipe. One last note—this is outstanding before, during, or after a meal of roast duck. The flavors marry in a remarkable way. Deep and rich. The 24 karat gold garnish is not overstated.

30 ml.	Rum, Bacardi *Black*
30 ml.	Coconut Rum, DeKuyper *Tropical Coconut*
10 ml.	Cointreau
20 ml.	Sherry, rich (*e.g.* Lustau *East India Solara*)
10 ml.	Lime juice, fresh
10 ml.	Orange juice, fresh
2 each	Allspice berries, freshly crushed
7-10 drops	Fine Balsamic Vinegar - see note above

Shake ingredients with ice, then strain through a fine mesh sieve to remove the allspice fragments. Always serve this straight up. For an extra touch of elegance, garnish with edible 24K gold leaf.

<u>Deception</u>

Brilliant! A very intriguing aperitif. The flavors of amaretto, strawberry and Campari mingle with the gin in a most curious way. Although there is nothing to suggest it in the list of ingredients, this cocktail is well suited before an Indian curry dish. The strawberry syrup that I prefer is Garden brand made in Poland. If you live in the United States, you may consider making your own syrup using fresh strawberries. Unfortunately American strawberries are usually lacking in flavor. You might also consider using Knott's Berry Farm strawberry syrup (sold in most American supermarkets). The flavor is more sugar than strawberries, but it is inexpensive, readily available, and will work. The Polish brand contains 30% actual strawberry juice and concentrated strawberry flavoring, and so strong that it counterbalances the highly-potent Campari. Exact measuring is especially important here (see page 43).

45 ml.	Gin, Bulldog
20 ml.	Amaretto Disaronno
1 teaspoon	Campari
40 ml.	Orange juice, fresh
10 ml.	Lime juice, fresh
1 teaspoon	Strawberry Syrup - see note above

Combine the ingredients and shake with a lot of ice. You want this slightly diluted and very cold. Strain into a chilled martini glass. I like to garnish this with a wedge of candied pineapple, to help disguise the secret ingredients (thus the name of the drink). If you want to give away the strawberry component, then you can garnish this with a fresh strawberry that has been macerated in syrup, but then increase the lime juice.

<u>Molotov Coqteez</u>

This drink is also very deceptive. It seems like a lot of

whiskey, even though there is only a trace. I think of this as a girl's whiskey cocktail. A certain type of girl. You probably know the kind I mean. Do *not* use canned grapefruit juice in this cocktail (or anywhere else for that matter, but *especially* not here). It must be freshly squeezed ruby grapefruit. For more about grapefruit, see Chapter 2.

40 ml.	Gin, Beefeater
20 ml.	Cognac, *VS*
30 ml.	Italian Vermouth, Martini *Rosso*
30 ml.	Ruby Grapefruit juice, fresh - see note above
10 ml.	Lemon juice, fresh
10 ml.	Sour Cherry Syrup (see notes on page 165)
4-6 drops	Peychaud's Bitters
	or substitute Angostura bitters (different but good)

Combine all ingredients and shake with ice. Pour into a chilled highball glass along with some of the ice cubes. Then float:

1 teaspoon	Whiskey, Jack Daniels

Serve with a sip straw. The garnish that I suggest for this drink is three cherries on a long skewer. Use cherries that have been soaked in either whiskey or brandy ahead of time.

G+L Cubed

Here is the old *Gin and Lime* cocktail reinvented on a whole new level. In my experience, everyone who likes gin and lime will find this drink fascinating and even amazing. You might imagine that this drink will be very sweet between the Cointreau and the maple syrup, but the grapefruit zest adds so much sourness that the sweeter components are there mostly to compensate, resulting in an intense flavor burst of citrus with a subliminal background note of the maple sugar.

60 ml.	Gin, Beefeater - doctored (page 65)
20 ml.	Lime juice, fresh
¾ teaspoon	Grapefruit Zest - see directions below
20 ml.	Cointreau
1 teaspoon	Maple Syrup

Grate the grapefruit zest into a fine mesh strainer, then slowly pour over the lime juice, followed by the gin. Press down on the zest to express as much of the liquid as possible. Discard the zest. Add the other ingredients. Shake with twice the usual amount of ice for about twice as long as you usually do. This should be diluted by the ice some, and *very* cold. Strain into a chilled glass, either on the rocks or straight up, as desired.

Yellow Diamond

This gives the impression of being stronger than it actually is when served straight-up, but the edge can be taken off by pouring it over ice.

40 ml.	Gin, Hendrick's
15 ml.	Light Rum, 10 Cane

¹/₂ teaspoon	Grapefruit Zest - see directions below
30 ml.	Orange juice, fresh
10 ml.	Lemon juice, fresh
10 ml.	Passion Fruit Syrup, homemade (page 100)
	or substitute Fee Bros. Golden Passion Fruit Syrup

Put the grated zest into a fine mesh strainer and slowly pour the gin over it. Press to extract as much of the gin as possible, then discard the zest. Combine the other ingredients and shake gently with ice. Garnish with a lemon wedge. Strain into a chilled cocktail glass, or pour it into a chilled highball glass with a sip straw.

Strawberry Roll

This was inspired by the *Stoli Roll*, an award winning cocktail from a bar in Hermosa Beach, California. This is made with better ingredients than most bars would consider using. The result is well worth going that extra mile for. Instead of using Stoli's Vanilla Vodka, I use a premium quality Russian vodka that has had a vanilla bean or two sliced and left to infuse for a minimum of two weeks. In a pinch you can add real vanilla extract to a good vodka, but the flavor will not be as good. I never use bottled sweet and sour mix, so in lieu of that foul concoction there is lemon juice and the hand crafted pomegranate syrup described earlier in this book. With the strawberries, the pomegranate produces a more harmonious flavor than simple syrup would. Ripe muddled strawberries are essential, so this drink can only be made when they are in season.

45 ml.	Vodka, Vanilla Infused - see note above
30 ml.	Lemon juice, fresh
15 ml.	Pineapple juice
10 ml.	Cranberry juice
10 ml.	Pomegranate Syrup (page 79)
2 small	Strawberries, fresh and very ripe - see below

Substitute one larger strawberry if you must, but smaller ones tend to be sweeter and more intensely flavored. Muddle the strawberries in the bottom of the shaker with the lemon juice. Add the rest of the ingredients and shake with ice. Strain into a chilled martini glass.

<u>Red Mercury</u>

Named after cinnabar, an ore of mercury similar in color. This drink is particularly well suited before Middle Eastern cuisine, or roasted lamb. This is one of those rare exceptions in which pomegranate molasses is actually used—as described earlier in the section on making Pomegranate Syrup (page 79). Since Cuban rum is not available in the United States as of the time of this writing. I suggest substituting Matusalem *Platino* Cuban style rum.

50 ml.	Vodka, Vanilla Infused - see previous recipe
20 ml.	Light Rum, Cuban - see note above

1 teaspoon	Cognac
15 ml.	Lemon juice, fresh
1 teaspoon	Pomegranate Molasses - see note above
1 teaspoon	Pomegranate Syrup (page 79)

Shake with ice and strain into a chilled martini glass. To further enhance this, sprinkle lightly with pure powdered sun dried vanilla bean (available online).

Orange Dynamite

Powerful, as the name forewarns. Although Monin's *Caribbean* syrup works fine in this, you might prefer the results obtained with your own spice syrup (page 106). Anyone who likes strong rum drinks should try this one.

25 ml.	Gin, London Dry
25 ml.	Rum, Jamaican Appleton *Special* or *X/V*
1/2 teaspoon	Orange Zest - see directions below
25 ml.	Lemon juice, fresh
25 ml.	Pineapple juice
15 ml.	Spiced Syrup (page 106)
	or substitute Monin *Caribbean* syrup
4-5 drops	Angostura Bitters

Grate the zest into a fine mesh strainer and gather it together into a small clump. Slowly pour over the gin, then the rum. Pinch the zest and press it against the mesh of the strainer to expel as much of the liquid as possible. Discard the zest and combine the rum and gin with the rest of the ingredients to a shaker. Shake with ice and strain into a decorative glass, such as a hand blown colored margarita style glass. Float on top:

25 ml.	Rum, Ron Zacapa *23 year*
	or another fine, smooth gold rum of your choosing

Lychee Martini

This drink was the signature cocktail at the restaurant Nonya, in Pasadena. Nonya had the distinction of being one of the only restaurants in all of America to specialize in Peranakan cuisine, also sometimes called Nonya cuisine. It is best described as a blend of Chinese, Indonesian and Malaysian styles, seldom seen outside of Singapore and Malaysia. Note that while this recipe duplicates the flavor of their signature cocktail perfectly, their actual recipe was never revealed to me. Just about everyone who ever tried this cocktail raved about it on blogs and reviews. Make it and see why!

70 ml.	Vodka, premium quality
20 ml.	Pineapple Juice
20 ml.	Lychee Syrup (page 101)
1 teaspoon	Vermouth, Cinzano *Bianco*
1 teaspoon	Lime Juice, fresh
10 drops	Orange Flower Water (optional)

Garnish with a canned lychee on a toothpick or skewer, in

the style of an olive in a martini. Use a quality brand of lychees, as the inferior brands are mushy and watery.

East India Bicycle Club Cocktail

The origin of this drink is a restaurant that went out of business several decades ago. This was one of the only good things on their menu, and the bar would be packed with patrons ordering this. A restaurant can not survive on the profits of a single drink though, no matter how popular. There were better restaurants on the same block, so savvy locals would get their name on a waiting list at one of the other nearby restaurants, then head to the East India Bicycle Club for one or two of these cocktails, then leave. So the bar was packed, while the rest of the restaurant was empty.

40 ml.	Gin, Plymouth
30 ml.	Apricot Brandy, Hiram Walker
15 ml.	Mango Schnapps, Hiram Walker
1 teaspoon	Cognac
1 Tablespoon	Apricot Curry Puree - see recipe below
15 ml.	Lemon juice, fresh
15 ml.	Monin *Curaçao Triple Sec* syrup

Combine all ingredients and shake with ice. Strain into a chilled martini glass and garnish with a strip of orange peel twisted around a long sliver of sugar cane.

The Apricot Curry Puree is prepared by blending canned

apricots with a little of their packing juice and hot Madras curry. I suggest about a teaspoon of curry powder for every half cup of apricots, but it will depend on the exact type of curry powder used, and personal taste. The resulting curry apricot puree should be stored in a refrigerator for at least a full day before using, and shaken well at least twice during this time. This will give the curry powder a chance to perfume the thick mixture and mellow slightly.

If you prefer, fresh apricots can be cooked with water, sugar and curry powder for about half an hour. Pass the mixture through a food mill with the finest mesh plate and discard the small amount of solids left behind. The resulting cocktail has a kick to it from the curry. The overall taste is sophisticated and unique.

<u>Spanish Coast and Spanish Fly</u>

The *Spanish Coast* here is almost identical to our version of the classic *Spanish Fly* cocktail. All you have to do is substitute tequila for the gin in this recipe. There have been countless versions of the Spanish Fly recipe published over the years. The most common version is simply Licor 43 and tequila (equal parts). Some recipes attempt to get around the Licor 43 component (since it can be difficult to find) with various combinations of ingredients such as butterscotch schnapps, orange and cola sodas, vanilla vodka, etc. Every one of these alternative versions that I have tasted were like sweetened cough syrup. The recipe shown below is not traditional, but it is quite delicious and still true to the integrity of the classic. Having said that, you should certainly try the Spanish Coast version of this drink (with gin). This is one of those cocktails that leaves people wondering what could possibly be in it. Most Licor 43 cocktails are composed of only two or three ingredients, making it stand out by itself. In these two drinks, the other ingredients work together to form a harmonious chord. You may have difficulty finding *Licor 43* in liquor stores, but it is readily available online. This Spanish liqueur gets its name from the 43 ingredients that it contains. The flavor is sweet vanilla and orange with many layers of herbal notes. Torani syrups may be purchased online, too.

60 ml.	Licor 43 liqueur - see note above
45 ml.	Spanish Brandy, Torres *10 Year*
30 ml.	Gin, Hendricks (or Tequila - see note above)
30 ml.	Orange Curaçao, Marie Brizard
30 ml.	Lemon juice, fresh
30 ml.	Lime juice, fresh
10 ml.	Pink Grapefruit Syrup, Torani
4-5 drops	Angostura bitters

Shake with ice and strain into glass. Garnish the *Spanish Coast* with candied lemon peel spiral wrapped around a cherry on a swizzle stick.

Elephant's Milk

This dessert drink is based on the classic *Voodoo* cocktail with slightly different proportions and replacing the Butterscotch Schnapps with a mixture of dark rum and natural brown sugar syrup. Also note that this is completely unrelated to the 19th century Elephant's Milk syrup preparation shown on page 253.

20 ml.	Coconut Rum, DeKuyper *Tropical Coconut*
20 ml.	Kahlúa liqueur
15 ml.	Dark Rum, Bacardi *Black*
1 teaspoon	Natural Brown Sugar Syrup (page 53)
60 ml.	Milk

Pour all ingredients over ice into a highball glass, and stir well. Add a sipping straw.

Pear Martini

My first exposure to this drink was at a restaurant in *The Grove*, next to the Farmer's Market in Los Angeles.

70 ml.	Pear Vodka, Grey Goose *La Poire*
20 ml.	Mathilde Pear Liqueur
10 ml.	Lime juice, fresh
1 teaspoon	Cointreau

Combine all ingredients and shake with ice. Strain into a chilled martini glass. Garnish with a thin slice of fresh pear.

<u>Starfruit Martini</u>

Starfruit, or carambola, are a delicious fruit native to Sri Lanka and Indonesia. Sliced across, each piece is star shaped.

40 ml.	Light Rum, Trinidad
30 ml.	Vodka
$^{1}/_{2}$ teaspoon	Creme de Banana, Bols
20 ml.	Lime juice, fresh
15 ml.	Starfruit Syrup (page 101)
3-4 drops	Complexing Agent #4 (page 241)

Combine all ingredients and shake with ice. Strain into a chilled martini glass that has been lined with paper thin slices of starfruit from the preparation of the starfruit syrup (page 101). The glass should have a circle of stars lining the sides.

HERBS IN COCKTAILS

<u>Eleganza</u>

This is a wonderful aperitif at a cocktail party. The key to this is *Amaro Nonino*, which might mean shopping online if you are in the United States. It has flavors of bitter orange and herbs. Unusual shaped small ice cubes are a nice touch.

30 ml.	Gin, Bombay *Sapphire*
20 ml.	Light Rum, 10 Cane
15 ml.	Amaro Nonino (an Italian liqueur)
20 ml.	Lemon juice, fresh

1 teaspoon	Monin *Triple Sec Curaçao* syrup
1/4 teaspoon	Brown Sugar
2 whole	Basil leaves, fresh - see directions below.

Put the lemon juice, sugar and basil into a shaker and muddle the basil well. Add the remaining ingredients. Shake with ice and strain off the basil leaf. Serve straight up in a chilled glass, then add small ice cubes. Silicone molds make it easy.

Rosemary-Tini

This is reminiscent of the *Rosemary's Baby* cocktail at Tavern on the Park. They make their own rosemary syrup, so that drinks can be simply poured. Heat changes the flavor, but preparing this fresh is time consuming. I have experimented with this many times and there is a more delicate balance involved here than you might guess.

60 ml.	Gin, Hendrick's
30 ml.	Apple juice
1 teaspoon	Lemon juice, fresh
1 teaspoon	Monin *Triple Sec Curaçao* syrup or substitute simple syrup (not as good)
1/4 teaspoon	Absinthe or substitute Pernod
1 teaspoon	Rosemary, minced - see directions below

Place the rosemary into a fine mesh strainer and drizzle the gin over it. Collect the gin and pour it over the rosemary herb a second time. Press the herb to get as much of the liquid out as possible. Combine the rest of the ingredients and shake with ice. Strain into a chilled martini glass. Garnish with a sprig of fresh rosemary, if desired.

Chartreuse Aperitif

This was created originally as the signature cocktail for a restaurant named Chartreuse. When new owners bought this popular place, they immediately changed the menu and dropped this drink entirely for being too complicated. I protested, pointing out that nearly half of their sales at the bar were for this one cocktail. They went out of business a few months later. This is a bewitching drink, especially in the right atmosphere.

20 ml.	Chartreuse Liqueur, *Green*
15 ml.	Gin, Tanqueray *Ten*
15 ml.	Vodka
15 ml.	Lemon juice, fresh
10 ml.	Orgeat Syrup, Trader Vic's
$^1/_2$ teaspoon	Thyme leaves, fresh - see directions below
10 drops	Complexing Agent #4 (page 241)

Muddle the thyme leaves with the gin, then add the rest of the ingredients to the shaker. Shake with a little ice and strain into a frosty cold small (3 $^1/_2$ ounce "mini") martini glass. Float a very thin slice of lemon on top. Be sure to remove any seeds from the lemon slice. We have some art noveau yellow-green glasses that were made in the 1920's for this cocktail, which adds a nice touch—especially if your bar has some blacklights. This type of glass glows under UV light because it contains uranium. This antique glassware can be found at online auction sites, and it is less expensive than your guests would ever imagine. Among collectors this is referred to as *vaseline glass*, or *uranium glass*, so use those keywords when searching online. Production of this type of glassware essentially ended with the Cold War due to uranium availability problems, so any glass you find of this type is bound to be vintage.

Speaking of uranium and the Cold War, here comes the next chapter…

ဆ Ï ღ

Chapter 8

Russia: The New Frontier

"Necessity is the Mother (Russia) of Invention"

My first visit to St. Petersburg, Russia was back in 2001. Perestroika was still a recent memory and fine gourmet cuisine was the indulgence of spoiled capitalists. Russians were still satisfied by simply having enough to eat. Vodka was consumed straight up, without ice. In fact, many Russians believed that drinking mixed liquors in a cocktail would make a person sick. The theme of almost all cuisine and drink was *simplicity*. Boiled potatoes, plain cabbage, and sausage were the everyday staples. If you think about it, vodka tastes as close to water as any liquor can, and until lateley the availability of imported spirits was woefully lacking. For instance, tequila was simply nonexistent.

With dramatic improvements in the general economy during the 2000's, a new culture of food and spirits began to take root for the first time in this part of the world. St. Petersburg is the world's new frontier for fusion cuisine and novel cocktails, but the reasons for that are beyond the scope of this chapter. While the availability of imported goods has improved dramatically over these past few years, there are still some things that are hard to find. On the other hand, certain exotic ingredients are readily available. When was the last time you saw mamoncillo fruit from Colombia, or sawberry syrup for sale? One reason that I took up residence here is to see and write about the historic changes that are happening right now. For the first time in all of Russia's history, ordinary Russians are exploring new foods and drinks. Cocktails and classic dishes like lasagna are being tasted for the first time. A new food culture is emerging, and I will be writing more about that in the next book.

One of the most surprising things about Russia today is the availability of exotic fruits. There are weird fruits imported from the jungles of South America and Polynesia with names printed in Russian that do not appear in any Russian-to-English dictionary I have ever found— so I don't even know what they are. The availability of spirits and liqueurs is also good these days, although you do have to search around some. There are no one-stop shops for imported liquors.

As you might guess, vodka is the absolute best here. While some other nations in Eastern Europe also produce very fine vodkas, the best Russian vodkas are rarely exported. The *Russian Standard* vodka that you might have seen, clearly states "made for export" on the label for a reason. It is not as good as the domestic product. I can state this with certainty, having sampled the two side by side several times. The market for vodka in Russia is infinitely more competitive, which means lower prices for better product. Stores devote an entire aisle for different vodkas, nearly all being brands that you will never see outside of Russia. Some are flavored with local herbs and berries that provide an entire artist's palette of unfamiliar tastes to explore. These are very hard to find elsewhere, even by online shopping. They are not exported.

 beginchar

EASTERN EUROPEAN LIQUORS

I have avoided providing recipes here that call for ingredients that are exceedingly difficult to procure. The spirits used here are popular enough that they are available online in most of the United States and Europe. I have selected one of the most useful spirits from each region…

> Lapponia Lingonberry (Finland)
>
> Vana Tallinn (Estonia)
>
> Riga Black Balsam (Latvia)
>
> Cedar Nut *eau de vie* (Russia)
>
> Vinjak (Serbia)

LAPPONIA LINGONBERRY LIQUEUR

Made in Finland, along with several other flavors made by the same company, and most being in identical bottles. Their Blueberry liqueur has been previously mentioned in this book (page 190). Lingonberry liqueur is an especially useful cocktail flavoring. It is sweet, but not nearly as sweet as most liqueurs. The flavor can be described as cherries mixed with cranberries, but without any of the tannic aftertaste of cranberry juice. Lapponia also produces Cloudberry and Buckthorn flavors, both being berries found only in Arctic

regions. The alcohol content of all of Lapponia's liqueurs is 21%, which is in the same range as port wine.

Finlandia Moonlight

This drink is loosely based on the classic Moonlight Cocktail which contains gin, white wine, grapefruit juice and cherry brandy. It has been given more of a tropical sweet & sour treatment here with the syrup and lemon juice.

60 ml.	Gin, Beefeater (doctored as previously described)
40 ml.	Lapponia Lingonberry liqueur
40 ml.	White Wine, dry
30 ml.	Lemon juice, fresh
$1/2$ teaspoon	Lemon Zest - see directions below
1 teaspoon	Grapefruit Juice, fresh
15 ml.	Monin *Amaretto* Syrup
	or substitute Orgeat Syrup

Grate the zest onto a fine mesh strainer and drizzle the lemon juice over it. Press to get as much of the liquid through as possible. Discard the zest and add the rest of the ingredients. Shake with ice and strain into a chilled white wine glass.

Lingo-Cosmo (Lingonberry Cosmopolitan)

Cranberries and lingonberries are related flavors, so it was a natural adaptation for Finland. Using Finlandia vodka would be a nice touch in this drink if you were writing a restaurant menu, but personally I stick to Russian Standard vodka most of the time.

60 ml.	Vodka
30 ml.	Lapponia Lingonberry liqueur
20 ml.	Lime juice, fresh
15 ml.	Cointreau

Shake with ice and strain into a chilled martini glass. Garnish with a twist of orange peel.

<u>Cloudberry 9</u>

This calls for Lapponia's Cloudberry liqueur, and although you can make it with their Lingonberry product, I do not suggest this. Cloudberry has a unique flavor that is indescribable. This is quite an unusual creamy drink, and a perennial favorite for after meals.

35 ml.	Lapponia Cloudberry - see note above
20 ml.	Vodka, Russian Standard
20 ml.	Light Rum, Havana Club *3 Year*
$3/4$ teaspoon	Crème de Noyaux
20 ml.	Pineapple juice
10 ml.	Heavy Cream

Combine all ingredients and shake vigorously with ice. Strain into a chilled martini glass straight up, or into a highball glass along with two or three of the ice cubes from the shaker, if you prefer.

All of Lapponia's liqueurs offer novel and pleasing flavors without being thick and cloying the way that most traditional liqueurs are.

<u>VANA TALLINN</u>

One of my absolute favorite liqueurs in Eastern Europe is *Vana Tallinn*. Curiously, it is sold in three concentrations, being distinguished by the alcohol level (40%, 45% and 50%). The 50% is the most intensely flavored, and also the hardest to find. It is quite sweet with strong notes of vanilla and orange in the nose, and a long finish of freshly grated nutmeg and clove, trailing off to a hint of anise and finally 15-20 seconds later a faint aftertaste of cinnamon candy. In terms of cocktails, this is a wonderful ingredient that every mixologist would love. If you are living in the United States, you will probably only find this through Internet shopping. Vana Tallinn is only available in certain parts of Europe. Hopefully its popularity will spread.

If you make your own vanilla ice cream, try using some Vana Tallinn as a flavoring component along with a little vanilla extract. The result is fabulous. It takes vanilla to a whole new level. If you can choose, then use the 40% alcohol variety, because less alcohol will have the least effect on the physical structure of the ice cream. I suggest two or three tablespoons per pint.

Hollywood Tallinn

Hollywood is a famous club in Tallinn, Estonia (adjacent to western Russia). After having lived in Hollywood, California, for many years, the name caught my attention. The music is loud and thumping, and the women are dangerously young and beautiful. *Vodka Vera* from Estonia has a girl from Tallinn on the label.

50 ml.	Vodka (*Vodka Vera* is nice, but hard to find)
20 ml.	Gin
15 ml.	Vanna Tallinn, *45% alcohol*
1 teaspoon	Cherry Brandy (liqueur), Marie Brizard
10 ml.	Vermouth, sweet Italian (Martini *Rosso*)
25 ml.	Orange juice, fresh

Combine all ingredients. Shake with ice and strain into a chilled Collins glass with enough of the ice to fill the glass. Top with the squeeze of fresh lime juice, and (if desired) garnish with a lime wedge.

The next two recipes are attempts at recreating two of my favorite drinks described earlier in this book, using ingredients that are available in St. Petersburg.

Russian Tiki Bowl

This is another relative of the *Scorpion* (see previous chapter) that has been optimized here for ingredients that are readily available in Russia. Vana Tallinn has notes of vanilla and almond that have been exploited in this recipe. The result is excellent, though it still pales in comparison to the more complex recipe shown on page 135.

40 ml.	Orange juice, fresh
25 ml.	Lemon juice, fresh
40 ml.	Gin, Beefeater - doctored (page 65)
$^1\!/_2$ teaspoon	Grapefruit zest (see directions below)
20 ml.	Cognac
10 ml.	Rum, Bacardi *Black*
10 ml.	Rum, Jamaican, Appleton *Special*
20 ml.	Amaretto, Disaronno
10 ml.	Vana Tallinn, *50% alcohol*
$^1\!/_2$ teaspoon	Pomegranate Syrup (page 79)

Pour the gin and the cognac over the grapefruit zest in a sieve, then discard the zest before continuing. Combine the rest of the ingredients. Shake with ice and serve on the rocks.

<u>Snow Maiden</u>

Based on the *Christmas Island* cocktail described earlier (page 167). The Russian fairytale Christmas characters are a Snow Maiden and Grandfather Frost, rather than Santa Claus. Benedictine is almost impossible to obtain in Russia, though I have no idea why since many other European liqueurs are plentiful.

30 ml.	Vana Tallinn, *45% alcohol*
25 ml.	Barbados Rum, R.L. Seales *10 Year*
10 ml.	Coconut Rum, Malibu
10 ml.	Cognac
1 teaspoon	Apricot Cognac (page 69)
30 ml.	Pineapple juice
25 ml.	Lemon juice, fresh
6-8 drops	Complexing Agent #3 (page 241)

Shake with ice and serve straight-up in a martini glass.

You might think pineapple juice and rum don't seem very Russian, but the nobles had anything they wanted imported to their dining table. The desire to impress guests with exotic imported foods and wines was the tradition of nobility and financiers throughout Europe for centuries. Within recent memory tropical fruits were scarce here, so their sudden availability has been enthusiastically welcomed. These days most stores have two entire aisles stocked with fruit juices!

<u>Tsarskoe Punch</u>

This drink is even better when prepared in a larger quantity and left in a punch bowl for a while. The centuries-old wisdom of letting punches rest before serving is often forgotten in modern recipes. Drinks with pieces of fresh fruit are usually best with punch bowl service. Ideally use a single ice sculpture in the center of the bowl to cool it down, because small ice cubes melt quickly and dilute it—or for single servings, put it in the freezer for about 20 minutes. Slice the orange and lemon *paper thin,* and then cut each round in half. Slices should remain suspended in the middle of the drink. Do not shake, or fruit will disintegrate.

30 ml.	Vodka, Russian Standard
30 ml.	Light Rum, Ron Varadero *Dry Silver*
30 ml.	White Wine, dry
15 ml.	Vana Tallinn, *45% alcohol*
10 ml.	Cointreau, or Triple Sec
30 ml.	Pineapple juice
20 ml.	Lemon juice, fresh
2 slices	Orange and Lemon, fresh - see notes above
1 teaspoon	Monin *Triple Sec Curaçao* syrup
	or substitute simple syrup

See notes above on refrigeration. Ladle into punch glasses.

COGNAC & VINJAK

Cognac is second only to vodka in popularity in Russia. The majority of the cognac consumed is actually produced in Armenia. Such Armenian cognac has a rating on each bottle of 1, 3, 5, 7 or 10 stars. Three and five star cognacs are the most popular because they are surprisingly drinkable at a low price. Armenian cognac has a distinctive flavor that is different from its French counterpart. There is less depth, and taste dissipates more rapidly on the palate. There are also some background spice notes that are unique to Armenian cognacs. I use the 7-star variety in some cocktails, and many Russians who are used to the distinctive flavor will pick up on that component in a cocktail, even when it is only a small amount in a complex recipe.

What I prefer in some cocktails is *Vinjak* from Croatia, such as that made by Cezar. Vinjak is also related to French cognac in the process, but due to some legal technicalities in the definition of what can be called "cognac" they were forced to choose a different name, and so Vinjak was born. In Russia this is uncommon, but not expensive and very well worth seeking out. It plays very well in cocktails because it lacks the harsh edge that Armenian cognacs have, and it is does not overpower other components. For most mixed drinks, my cognac of choice is still Hennessy *VSOP*, though. The main problem is that in Russia the price of Hennessy is

"

several times as much as in the United States. Some recipes actually work better with Vinjak, because of its subtle notes of black peppercorns. For example, the *North Market Mango Cocktail* (see page 105).

Nearly every Russian hates ice in drinks, and that includes cocktails. Beer is served only slightly chilled. This common sentiment is probably due to the cold of Russian winter.

Susanushka

A five-star Turkish resort cocktail for 21st century Eastern Europe. Served slightly warm, this is a memorable libation.

45 ml.	Vinjak, Cezar
	or substitute Cognac (different, but also good)
20 ml.	Grand Marnier
25 ml.	Orange juice, fresh
1 teaspoon	Lemon juice, fresh
1/2 teaspoon	Orange Zest - see directions below
1 teaspoon	Demerara Sugar or Palm Sugar

Muddle the zest with the sugar and both citrus juices. Warm in a pan of hot water until steaming. Add the two liquors, then strain off the zest. Serve in a large decorative glass wine goblet. Garnish with a dash of freshly grated Star Anise.

RIGA BLACK BALSAM

Angostura and other popular cocktail bitters are virtually unknown in Eastern Europe. Cocktails themselves are still largely a novelty from recent exposure to Western culture. Bear in mind that there is no cocktail heritage here, or Tiki culture. Hawaii was never promoted as a tourist destination to Russians. James Michner's *South Pacific* never made it here—the book, the musical, or even the movie. There was never a single Tiki bar in Soviet Russia. For that matter, even the quintessentially cool James Bond sipping his shaken-not-stirred *Vesper Martini* is an alien concept. When Russians do order a cocktail today, they are usually talking about vodka mixed with some fruit juice or soda. Generally speaking, drinking straight liquor is a sign of manliness, just as it was for Americans in the past.

However, there are a few aperitifs like Black Balsam (pictured here) that certainly qualify as bitters. It is hard to imagine how anyone can drink this stuff straight, but then personally I would say the same thing about Campari.

I put them both in the same category. They are fabulous in small portions, but can easily overwhelm. In more recent times, as culinary sophistication grows here, Black Balsam is being added in small portions to cocktails by Russians in the same way that Angostura and Peychaud's are used elsewhere.

One of my favorite brands in the United States is Fee Bros. These bitters do not seem to exist in Russia, and so I had to find what else could be used instead. Pouring a drink that contains Black Balsam over orange zest produces an impersonation of *Orange Bitters*. Just as Black Balsam with grapefruit zest does an impersonation of *Grapefruit Bitters*. The next recipe demonstrates this…

<u>1917 Cocktail</u>

This is the mutant monster brother of a *Leon Trotsky* cocktail, which is composed of vodka, tequila and raspberry liqueur. This has a magnificantly complex flavor. The *1917* evolved over several years until it became something almost unrecognizable from the original *Leon Trotsky*. This is too much trouble for most bars to make, but highly recommended if you want something that is really interesting. This is another drink that will stump anyone as to what is in it, although the tequila and vodka still manage to shine through, despite being minor components. There are flavor overtones of the Margarita, which is really impossible to avoid for any cocktail that contains lime and tequila. Cranberry syrup is something available in every grocery store in Russia. There are many sources of this syrup online. As with other complex recipes, pay careful attention so as not to leave out any ingredient.

40 ml.	Gin
20 ml.	Cognac, Armenian *7-star*
15 ml.	Vodka
10 ml.	Tequila
20 ml.	Lime juice, fresh
15 ml.	Grapefruit juice, fresh
15 ml.	Cranberry Syrup (*not* cranberry juice)
1 teaspoon	Black Balsam

Combine all ingredients. Put the following into a fine mesh sieve:

$^1/_2$ teaspoon	Lime Zest
$^1/_4$ teaspoon	Grapefruit Zest

Pour the previous mixture over the zests slowly. Press the zests to express as much of the liquid as possible. Shake well with a cup of ice, then strain into a chilled cocktail glass.

This is also known as "Cedar Nut Eau de vie" in other parts of Europe. This is not a sweet liqueur. It is traditional drink made from Russian vodka that has been infused with a special kind of cedar nuts that grow in a pristine region of the Taiga forest in Northern Siberia. It is readily available in Russia, slightly hard to find in the rest of Europe, and very difficult to find in the United States—but worth the effort for the intrepid mixologist. This is a great "secret weapon" for preparing signature cocktails, or just to add

in trace amounts for dousing customized liquor (page 56). Cedar Nut Vodka is unlike any other spirit I have tried. It plays especially well with gin, vodka and many liqueurs. Because it is a Russian product dating back hundreds of years, and only now are Russians becoming enlightened about mixing cocktails, it is still customary to drink it straight as an apertif. I do not suggest this, other than as a learning experience to familiarize yourself with its flavor profile. Most people would say that it is quite unpleasant tasting by itself, being slightly reminiscent of pine scented room freshener. This character changes when mixed with other ingredients. It will not dominate a cocktail the way that some spirits do (such as tequila, for example). Cedar Nut Vodka can remain in the background of an orchestra of flavors. I think of it as cedar bitters that have been substantially diluted in vodka. Cedar Bitters were actually produced and sold in the 19th century. The alcohol content is the same as Russian vodka (38-40%).

Dacha Punch

Russians in St. Petersburg spend weeks, or even months every summer at their dacha, or summer house. Dachas are located one to two hours by car outside of the city and better dachas have a banya, or sauna. This cocktail was created for the summer house of a wealthy friend here. Warning: this is a seriously potent punch! See notes on previous recipe regarding cranberry syrup. When scaling this recipe up for more people, note that 1 teaspoon is 5 ml.

75 ml.	Vodka, Russian
25 ml.	Cedar Nut Vodka
10 ml.	Italian Vermouth, Martini *Rosso*
50 ml.	Orange juice, fresh
2 thin slices	Lime, fresh - see diretions below
1 teaspoon	Cranberry Syrup (*not* cranberry juice)

Combine all ingredients and stir. Store in the refrigerator for at least an hour, and preferably several hours before service.

<u>Zdravo</u>

The story goes that three friends went hunting bears somewhere in the far north. There was a Russian, a Croatian and a Frenchman. Each brought one bottle of liquor along. One night they pooled their liquid assets and created this drink. This is a good example of how cedar nut vodka can play a background role. It modifies the flavor of the calvados to produce a simple Old World style cocktail that evokes images of dark European forests. Note that the original drink was simply equal parts calvados, vodka and cedar nut vodka and no ice. I have yet to find the person who does not prefer this version of the recipe instead…

40 ml.	Calvados
30 ml.	Vodka
20 ml.	Cedar Nut Vodka
10 ml.	Lemon juice, fresh
10 ml.	Natural Brown Sugar Syrup (page 53)

Combine all ingredients in a glass with cracked ice, and stir well.

<u>FLAVORED VODKAS</u>

The practice of infusing vodka with berries and herbs goes back centuries in Russia. Some traditional flavors are now bottled and sold commercially, but not exported. Some flavors are produced at home, because they taste best when freshly made.

<u>Pavlovsk Cocktail</u>

Named after Pavlovsk Palace. *Podvorye*, one of the most famous restaurants of St. Petersburg is just the street from the palace. Bayberries are sold in small packages at grocery stores in Russia, but are only available by Internet shopping in most other countries. One source is efooddepot.com

100 ml.	Vodka, Russian
1 Tablespoon	Bayberries, dried - see note above
10 ml.	Lemon juice, fresh
1 teaspoon	Monin *Triple Sec Curaçao* syrup

The vodka and the dried bayberries are combined and stored in a jar in the refrigerator for 3-5 days before use. Of course you can multiply the amount to prepare as much as you like ahead of time. Strain the vodka through a fine mesh strainer, and squeeze out the berries to get as much of the liquid as possible. Combine the bayberry flavored vodka with the syrup and lemon juice. Divide into shotglasses at room temperature (traditional), or shake with ice and serve cold.

<u>Horseradish Vodka</u>

This is served in *Restaurant Chekhov*, an important establishment in St. Petersburg that recreates the menu and dining experience of a dacha in the late 19th century. Russia is the land of contradictions in many ways. This is a good example of that. In a country where people consider black pepper as being a fiery hot spice in food, they seem to have no difficulty in consuming several shots of this corrosive apertif. Not that I don't enjoy it, but it seems peculiar that Russians who fear spice like a vampire fears garlic, would enjoy this delicacy.

200 ml.   Vodka, Russian
25 grams   Horseradish, fresh (peeled well and cubed)

Combine the vodka and horseradish in a jar and allow to steep in the refrigerator for 24 to 48 hours. If it is too strong, then dilute it back down with straight vodka. Strain off the horseradish and divide into shotglasses. Store these in the freezer for 30 minutes before serving. The liquid will turn slightly milky due to traces of oil from the horseradish coming out of the ice cold solution.

Although rum is not nearly as popular in Russia as vodka and cognac, just about every store carries Cuban rum. The two most popular are Havana Club's 3 year white rum, and their 7 year dark rum. Both are outstanding in cocktails. In fact the 3 year white rum is everything you could ever hope for in a light rum for mixing. Try an taste experiment by nibbling on a little 85% dark chocolate between sips of Havana Club 7 year dark rum and another dark rum of your choice. This will help you to see the unique characteristics of this rum more clearly.

There is a never ending debate about where rum was first invented. Several countries claim to be the birthplace of rum, but Cuba is often regarded as the winner in this feud since sugar cane was introduced there by Christopher Columbus back in 1493, and rum production soon followed. However the early days of rum production had little in common with today's highly refined products. Rum was being made on slave plantations, and it was common practice for the master of the plantation to empty his chamber pot into the fermenting liquor to discourage slaves from drinking from it. The idea was that it would be distilled later anyway, and so the human waste products would be left behind. Some even imagined that the bacteria in feces would help the fermentation go faster. Distillation may have sanitized the spirit, but the flavor was still tainted (at best). This is around the same time that rum was nicknamed Kill Devil, quite possibly from being so foul tasting that it would kill the Devil himself. Things did not get significantly better until the 19th century, when a world market for better tasting spirits had evolved and there was suddenly an incentive to produce liquor that would do more than get you hammered—it would actually taste good. A rum that would blend well in cocktails seems to have originated by direct request from Spanish royalty.

Unlike most other spirits, the rules for how "rum" can be made and still be called "rum" have never been well defined. Consequently there are several significantly different methods of production, and a wide array of differences between producers, even in the same region. Rums are frequently grouped by the country of production (*e.g.* a

Puerto Rican rum, or a Barbados rum, *etc.*) Although this is a broad generalization with many exceptions, there is really no other reasonable sorting method. The exact methods of production in different nations by different rum makers is a topic far too involved to undertake here.

Cuban rum owes its distinctive characteristics chiefly to the innovations established by Pedro Diago, a Cuban "Maestro Ronero" (master rum maker) who is regarded as the father of Cuban rum. One of his most important contributions was the unusual idea of burying containers of partially completed rum in the ground so that they would remain warm while they aged. The lighter flavorful style of rum, known as "Ron Superior" was first developed in Cuba on request for the royal family of Spain in the mid-19th century. The art of rum making has been serious business in Cuba for centuries now. Even moderately priced Cuban rums are quite smooth and have a lingering pleasant aftertaste that speaks of quality. One of the finest examples of Cuban rum is Ron Varadero's 15 year dark rum. This is available online in just about every nation of the world except the United States.

<u>SPICED RUM</u>

Quality spiced rum in Russia is scarce. When such a rum is needed for a recipe, necessity is once again the mother of invention. In my opinion, the following recipe is superior to any other commercial spiced rum that I have ever tasted.

50 ml.	Dark Rum, Bacardi *Black*
50 ml.	Light Rum, Havana Club *3 year*
10 ml.	Lemon juice, fresh
20 ml.	Spiced Syrup (page 106)
5-8 drops	Complexing Agent #2 (page 240)

Combine all ingredients. Refrigerate, or use immediately due to the fresh lemon juice present.

<u>RUSSIAN GIN</u>

What we think of as "gin" is a combination of juniper and certain herbs that have been infused in neutral grain spirits, better known as vodka. In terms of popularity in Russia, the order of preference is vodka, cognac, rum, and then gin. While there is a vodka flavored with juniper berries, without the other herbal components it has less in common with gin than you might imagine. Nearly all of the gin consumed in Russia is imported from England. The one notable exception is *Manhattan Gin*, produced and bottled in Russia. The name jumped out at me as humorous for the following reasons. First, a *Manhattan* cocktail contains no gin. Second, fine gins are usually from London, not New York City. Third, there is no actual city of Manhattan anywhere in Russia. The taste is difficult to describe, but it is actually quite drinkable straight. When it comes to

mixing cocktails with it, this is not something you are going to make a *Martini* with. It takes some playing with to find what kind of cocktail it actually can perform well in, because it has some peculiar flavor notes unlike anything else. Almost certainly due to some Russian herbs being used, rather than the traditional botanical components used in London gin. The following cocktail was created for this gin…

<u>Russian Gin and Rum Martini</u>

This is the only cocktail I have ever found that would be equally well presented with a garnish of either a stuffed olive or a maraschino cherry. Even if you never make this drink, that fact alone should give you some idea of just how unusual this is. While this drink may be prepared with any gin you like, this really works best with Russia's *Manhattan Gin*.

60 ml.	Gin, Russian *Manhattan*
20 ml.	Dark Rum, Havana Club *7 Year*
10 ml.	Vana Tallinn, *45% alcohol*
1/2 teaspoon	Black Balsam
10 ml.	Lime Juice, fresh

Combine all ingredients and stir with cracked ice gently. Strain into a chilled cocktail glass. Garnish with either a cherry or an olive (!) as discussed above.

◈ CONCLUSION ◈

At this point I have covered the middle ground that I sought to document at the start of this book. Namely, to fill that void between the simplistic, "mix these three things and serve cold" approach ubiquitous today, and those elaborate methods that were evolving into a complete science until the Great Depression struck (see page 109). From here the next level in creating unusual cocktails involves more complicated techniques. In my next book I will focus on the customized distillation of spirits using ordinary kitchen equipment.

ജ Y ങ

APPENDIX A

Metric Conversions

When converting to metric units, there are only two things you really need to remember. An ounce is about 30ml, and a teaspoon is about 5ml. Everything else is just simple math. This chart summarizes the most common conversions.

Ounces	Use	Precision
1/8 oz.	3/4 teaspoon	3.75 ml.
1/6 oz.	1 teaspoon	4.9 ml.
1/4 oz.	1 1/2 teaspoons	7.4 ml.
1/3 oz.	10 ml.	9.9 ml.
1/2 oz.	15 ml.	14.9 ml.
3/4 oz.	20 ml.	22.2 ml.
1 oz.	30 ml.	29.6 ml.
1 1/2 oz.	45 ml.	44.4 ml.
2 oz.	60 ml.	59.2 ml.
2 1/2 oz.	75 ml.	74 ml.
3 oz.	90 ml.	88.8 ml.
3 1/2 oz.	105 ml.	103.6 ml.

* The only significant error is in the case of 3/4 ounce, which is short by about 11%. You can fix this by adding another 1/2 teaspoon to the 20ml measured, which will reduce the error to an insignificant 0.3ml.

APPENDIX B

Complexing Agents

This is a quick and dirty compromise between fermenting and distilling your own spirits to obtain unique flavors, and just settling for what commercial manufacturers offer you.

These are powerful flavoring agents, but their strength is imprecise because there is no reliable way to obtain consistency in a home (or bar) environment. Their flavor develops over weeks, and variations in the room temperature and the nature of specific ingredients will influence the outcome, as well as the exact age. You do not remove the solids. You just pour off the liquid as you need it. Eventually when it runs dry, you discard the solids and start again. You will need to taste drinks that call for these periodically and adjust the amount of complex that you add accordingly.

In all cases, the optimum flavor will take about three months to fully develop. The quantity of Complexing Agent specified in the recipes in this book is only an approximation. It will depend on how developed the batch you are using is, and your own personal tastes. It is also difficult to measure these complexes in drops, because they pour in "threads" when they are fully developed.

I primarily use these four types of Complexing Agents described below, but you can make up your own, of course. They are all made the same way, with only the ingredients varying. Each must be stored for a prolonged period of time until it becomes thick and syrup-like in consistency. This means several weeks of storage. Use a small jar with no more than twice the portions stated here for any one batch. Baby food jars work well for this. Once fully developed, the solution will keep for a very long time. Keep it with the solids, though. If you strain off the liquid, it will begin to lose its potency quickly. The solids in the jar keep it charged.

Complexing Agent #1

Otherwise known as the Cocoa Complex.

30 ml.	Amaretto, Disaronno
1 teaspoon	Cocoa powder (99% cacao)
1/4 teaspoon	Cinnamon, ground
1 teaspoon	Grapefruit Zest

Combine all ingredients in a jar and store for at least two weeks, occasionally shaking the contents. This will gradually turn into a viscous fluid, like a thin honey.

Complexing Agent #2

The Caribbean Complex.

30 ml.	Rum

1 each	Nutmeg, whole (broken into pieces)
1 each	Cinnamon, stick (broken into pieces)
1 ½ teaspoons	Orange Zest

Combine all ingredients in a jar and store for at least two weeks, occassionally shaking the contents. This will gradually turn into a viscous fluid, like honey.

Complexing Agent #3

The Morocco Complex. Do *not* use black or brown cardamom pods in this. This complex is frequently chosen to compliment cocktails that contain Benedictine.

30 ml.	Cognac
½ teaspoon	Black Peppercorns, whole
5 each	Cardamom pods, whole (white or green)
2 teaspoons	Lemon Zest

Crush the peppercorns and cardamom pods lightly with a mortar and pestle before adding to the cognac and zest. Combine all ingredients in a jar and store for at least two weeks, occassionally shaking the contents. This will gradually turn into a viscous fluid, like honey.

Complexing Agent #4

Sometimes referred to as the Egyptian Complex.

| 40 ml. | Vodka |

1 teaspoon	Coriander seeds, whole
$^1/_2$ teaspoon	Allspice, whole
$^1/_2$ teaspoon	Fennel seeds, whole
pinch	Saffron threads, crumbled
1 teaspoon	Lime Zest

Crush the coriander, allspice and fennel seeds lightly with a mortar and pestle. Combine with other ingredients in a jar and store for at least two weeks, occassionally shaking the contents. This will gradually turn into a viscous fluid, like honey.

APPENDIX C

Selected 1928 Recipes

Caution: Do *not* make these recipes. Many are unsafe.

See page 109 for the introduction to this section.

4. CARAWAY BRANDY

Steep one ounce of caraway-seed and six ounces of loaf sugar with one quart of brandy. Let it stand nine days and then draw off.

5. BLACK CHERRY BRANDY

Stone two pounds of black cherries and put on them one quart of brandy. Bruise the stones in a mortar, and then add them to the brandy. Cover them close and let them stand a month or six weeks. Then pour it clear from the sediment and bottle it. Morello cherries, managed in this way, make a fine cordial.

6. CHERRY BRANDY

For this purpose use either morello cherries or small black cherries. Pick them from the stalks; fill the bottles nearly up to the necks, then fill up with brandy (some people use whiskey, gin, or spirit distilled from the lees of the wine.) In three weeks or a month strain off the spirit; to each quart add one pound of loaf sugar clarified, and flavor with tincture of cinnamon or cloves.

7. ORANGE BRANDY

Put the chips of six Seville oranges in one quart of brandy, and let them steep a fortnight in a stone bottle close stopped. Boil two and two-thirds pints of spring water with eight ounces of the finest sugar, nearly an hour, very gently. Clarify the water and sugar with the white of an egg; then strain it through a jelly-bag, and boil it nearly half away. When it is cold, strain the brandy into the syrup.

---

8. RASPBERRY BRANDY

Raspberry brandy is infused nearly after the same manner as cherry brandy, and drawn off with about the same addition of brandy to what is drawn off from the first, second, and third infusion, and dulcified accordingly, first making it of a bright deep color, omitting cinnamon and cloves in the first, but not in the second and third infusion. The second infusion will be somewhat paler than the first, and must be lightened in color by adding one pint cherry brandy, with five or more gallons of raspberry brandy, and the third infusion will require more cherry brandy to color it. It may be flavored with the juice of elderberry.

---

9. HOW TO PREPARE ESSENCE OF COGNAC

Take 1 ounce oil cognac—the green oil is the best; put it in $\frac{1}{2}$ gallon 95 per cent spirits. Cork it up tight, shake it frequently for about 3 days; then add 2 ounces strong ammonia. Let it stand 3 days longer; then place in a stone jar that will contain about 3 gallons, 1 pound fine black tea, 2 pounds prunes, having first mashed the prunes and broken the kernels. Pour on them 1 gallon spirits 20 above proof. Cover it close, and let it stand 8 days. Filter the liquor, and mix with that containing the oil and ammonia. Bottle it for use. This makes the best flavoring known for manufacturing brandies, or for adding to such cordials, syrups, etc., as require a fine brandy flavor.

◇—◇—◇

10. IMITATION COGNAC BRANDY

To 36 gallons French proof spirits, add 4 gallons Pellevoisin or Marette cognac, ½ gallon best sherry or Madeira wine, and 20 drops oil of cognac, dissolved in a little 95 per cent alcohol. Then pour 2 quarts boiling water over 2 ounces black tea; when cold, filter through flannel, and add a little maraschino; mix this with the other ingredients, and color the whole to suit, with caramel.

Another excellent formula is as follows: Dissolve 20 drops oil of cognac and 15 drops oil of bitter almonds in a little 95 per cent alcohol; add it to 40 gallons 60 per cent French spirit, with 2 pints tincture of raisin, 2 pints of tincture of prunes, 3 pints best Jamaica rum, 3 pints best sherry wine, and ½ ounce acetic ether. Color with caramel.

◇—◇—◇

11. IMITATION BRANDY

Take 40 gallons French spirit; add to it 1 pint tincture of raisins, 1 quart prune flavoring, ½ gallon best sherry or Madeira wine, and 1 pint wine vinegar. Then add 1 drachm oil of cognac, 12 drops oil of bitter almonds, ⅛ to ½ drachm tannin powder, each dissolved separately in 95 per cent alcohol. Color to suit with caramel.

---

12. IMITATION FRENCH BRANDY

To 40 gallons French proof spirit, add 1 quart tincture of orris root, 1 pint vanilla flavoring, ½ gallon best sherry or Madeira wine, and 1 pint wine vinegar. Dissolve separately, 1 drachm oil of cognac and 12 drops oil of bitter almonds, each in a little 95 per cent alcohol, and add them to the mixture, coloring the whole to suit with caramel.

---

13. IMITATION PALE BRANDY

Infuse 1 drachm star-anise (breaking the star only) for 8 hours in ½ pint 95 per cent alcohol, and filter; add this to 40 gallons proof spirits; then add ½ gallon best Jamaica rum, and 1 pint of the best raspberry syrup. Dissolve 1 drachm oil of cognac, and 12 drops oil of bitter almonds, separately, in a little 95 per cent alcohol and mix them with the whole.

20. CARAWAY CORDIAL

Take 1 teaspoonful of oil of caraway, four drops of cassia-lignea oil, 1 drop of essence of orange peel, 1 drop of essence of lemon, 5 quarts and a gill of spirits, 1¾ pounds of loaf sugar. Make it up and fine it down.

21. CITRON CORDIAL

½ pound yellow rind of citrons, 2 ounces orange peel, ⅓ ounce bruised nutmegs, 2⅙ gallons proof spirit; macerate, add water sufficient, and ½ pound of fine lump sugar for every gallon of the cordial.

22. CLOVE CORDIAL

Take ¼ of a pound of cloves, bruised, 1 ounce pimento, or allspice, 2 gallons proof spirit. Digest the mixture 12 hours in a gentle heat, and then draw off with a pretty brisk fire. The water may be colored red, either by strong tincture of cochineal, alkanet or corn poppy-flowers. It may be dulcified at pleasure with refined sugar.

23. CORIANDER CORDIAL

⅓ pound coriander seeds, ⅓ ounce of caraways, and the peel and juice of ½ orange to every gallon of proof spirit.

◇◇◇

24. GINGER CORDIAL

Pick 1 pound of large white currants from their stalks, lay them in a basin, and strew over them the rind of an orange and a lemon cut very thin, or ½ teaspoonful of essence of lemon, and 1 ounce and one-half of the best ground ginger, and 1 quart of good whiskey. Let all lie for 24 hours. If it tastes strong of the ginger, then strain it; if not, let it lie for 12 hours longer. To every quart of strained juice add 1 pound of loaf sugar pounded. When the sugar is quite dissolved, and the liquor appears clear, bottle it. This cordial is also extremely good made with raspberries instead of currants.

◇◇◇

25. LEMON CORDIAL

Pare off very thin the yellow rind of some fine lemons. Cut the lemons in half and squeeze out the juice. To each pint of the juice allow ½ pound of loaf sugar. Mix the juice, the peel, and the sugar together. Cover it and let it set 24 hours. Then mix it with an equal quantity of white brandy. Put it into a jug, and let it set a month. Then strain through a linen bag and afterward through blotting-paper before you bottle it.

26. LIME JUICE CORDIAL

Lime juice cordial that will keep good for any length of time may be made as follows: 6 pounds sugar, 4 pints water, 4 ounces citric acid, ½ ounce boric acid. Dissolve by the aid of a gentle heat, and when cold add 60 ounces refined lime juice, 4 ounces tincture of lemon peel, water to make up 2 gallons.

27. STRAWBERRY OR RASPBERRY CORDIAL

Sugar down the berries overnight, using more sugar than you would for the table, about half as much again. In the morning lay them in a hair sieve over the basin; let them remain until evening, so as to thoroughly drain. Then put the juice in a thick flannel bag; let it drain all night, being careful not to squeeze it, as that takes out the brightness and clearness. All this should be done in a cool cellar, or it will be apt to sour. Add brandy in the proportion of ⅓ the quantity of juice, and as much more sugar as the taste demands. Bottle it tightly. It will keep 6 to 8 years, and is better at last than at first.

28. WHISKEY CORDIAL

Take 1 ounce of cinnamon, 1 ounce of ginger, 1 ounce of coriander seed, ½ ounce of mace, ½ ounce of cloves, ½ ounce of cubebs. Add 3 gallons of proof spirit and 2½ quarts of water. Now tie up 1⅓ ounces of English saffron, 1 pound of raisins (stoned), 1 pound dates; 3 ounces licorice root. Let these stand 12 hours in 2½ quarts of water; strain, and add it to the above. Dulcify the whole with fine sugar.

29. ANISETTE DE BOURDEAUX

Take 9 ounces sugar, 6 drops aniseed. Rub them together and add, by degrees, 2 pints spirits of wine, 4 pints water. Filter.

30. CREME DES BARBADOES

Take 1 dozen middling sized lemons, 3 large citrons, 14 pounds loaf sugar, ¼ pound fresh balm leaves, 5 quarts spirits of wine, 7 quarts of water. Cut lemons and citrons in thin slices and put them into a cask, pour upon them the spirit of wine, bung down close, and let it stand 10 days or a fortnight; then break the sugar, and boil it for ½ hour in the water, skimming it frequently. Then chop the balm leaves, put them into a large pan, and pour upon them the boiling liquor, and let it stand till quite cold; then strain it through a lawn sieve, and put it to the spirits, etc., in the cask. Bung down close, and in a fortnight draw it off. Strain it through a jelly-bag and let remain to fine; then bottle it.

31. CREME DE NOYAU DE MARTINIQUE

Take 20 pounds of loaf sugar, 3 gallons of spirit of wine, 3 pints of orange-flower water, 1¼ pounds of bitter almonds, 2 drams of essence of lemon, 4½ gallons of water. The produce will exceed 8 gallons. Put 2 pounds of the loaf sugar into a jug or can, pour upon it the essence of lemon, and 1 quart of the spirit of wine. Stir till the sugar is dissolved, and the essence completely incorporated. Bruise the almonds and put them into a 4 gallon stone bottle or cask, add the remainder of the spirit of wine, and the mixture from the jug or can. Let it stand a week or ten days, shaking it frequently. Then add the remainder of the sugar, and boil it in the 4½ gallons of water for ¾ of an hour, taking off the scum as it rises. When cold, put in a cask; add the spirit, almonds, etc., from the stone bottle, and lastly the orange-water. Bung it down close and let it stand 3 weeks or a month; then strain it off in a jelly-bag, and when fine, bottle it off. When the pink is wanted, add cochineal, in powder, at the rate of ½ dram or two scruples to 1 quart.

32. CREME D'ORANGE OF SUPERIOR FLAVOR

Take 1 dozen middling sized oranges, 1¼ pints orange-flower water, 6 pounds loaf sugar, 2⅔ quarts spirit of wine, ½ ounce tincture of saffron, 4⅔ quarts water. Cut the oranges in slices, put them in a cask, add the spirit and orange-flower water, let it stand a fortnight. Then boil the sugar in the water for ½ hour, pour it out, and let it stand till cold; then add it to the mixture in the cask; and put in the tincture of saffron. Let it remain a fortnight longer; then strain, and proceed as directed in the recipe for Creme de Barbadoes, and a very fine cordial will be produced.

◇◇◇

33. EAU DE BARBADOES

Take 1 ounce of fresh orange peel, 4 ounces of fresh lemon peel, 1 dram coriander, 4 pints proof spirit. Distill in a bath heat, and add white sugar in powder.

◇◇◇

34. EAU DE BIGARADE

Take the outer or yellow part of the peels of seven bigarades (a kind of orange), ¼ ounce of nutmegs, ⅛ ounce of mace, ½ gallon of fine proof spirit, 1 quart of water. Digest all these together two days in a close vessel, after which draw off a gallon with a gentle fire, and dulcify with fine sugar.

◇◇◇

35. EAU DEVINE

Take ½ gallon of spirit of wine, ½ dram essence of lemons and ½ dram essence of bergamot. Distill in a bath heat, add 2 pounds sugar, dissolved in 1 gallon of pure water, and lastly 2½ ounces of orange-flower water.

36. ELEPHANT'S MILK

Take 2 ounces gum benzoin, 1 pint spirit of wine, 2½ pints boiling water. When cold, strain and add 1½ pounds sugar.

37. HUILE DE VENUS

Take 6 ounces of flowers of wild carrot, picked, 10 pints spirit of wine. Distill in a bath heat. To the spirit add as much syrup of Capillaire; it may be colored with cochineal.

38. LIGNODELLA

Take the thin peel of 3 oranges and 3 lemons; steep them in ½ gallon of brandy or rum, close stopped for 2 or 3 days. Then take 3 quarts of water and 1½ pounds of loaf sugar clarified with the whites of 2 eggs. Let it boil ¼ hour, then strain it through a fine sieve, and let it stand till cold; strain the brandy with the peels, add the juice of 3 oranges and 5 lemons to each gallon. Keep it close stopped up 5 weeks, then bottle it.

39. MARASCHINO

1 gallon proof whiskey, 2 quarts of water, dissolve 4 pounds of sugar, ⅓ dram oil of bergamot, ⅓ dram oil

of cloves, 2 drops oil of cinnamon, ⅔ ounce of nutmegs, bruised, 5 ounces of orange peel, 1 ounce of bitter almonds, bruised, ⅓ dram oil of lemon. Dissolve the oil in alcohol; color with cochineal and burnt sugar.

❖❖❖

40. MARASQUIN DE GROSEILLES

Take 8½ pounds of gooseberries, quite ripe, 1 pound black cherry leaves. Bruise and ferment; distill and rectify the spirits. To each pint of this spirit add as much distilled water, and 1 pound of sugar.

❖❖❖

41. NECTAR

Take 3 gallons of red ratafia, ¼ ounce of cassia-oil, and an equal quantity of the oil of caraway seeds. Dissolve in a little spirit of wine, and make up with orange wine so as to fill up the jug. Sweeten, if wanted, by adding a small lump of sugar in the glass.

❖❖❖

42. NOYAU

Take 1½ gallons of French brandy, 1 in 5, 6 ounces of the best French prunes, 2 ounces of celery, 3 ounces of the kernels of apricots, nectarines, and peaches, and 1 ounce of bitter almonds, all gently bruised, 2 pennyweights of essence of lemon peel, 1½ pounds of loaf

254

sugar. Let the whole stand 10 days or a fortnight. Then draw off, and add to the clear noyau as much rose-water as will make up to 2 gallons.

◇◇◇

43. RATAFIA

This is a liquor prepared from different kinds of fruits, and is of different colors, according to the fruits made use of. These fruits should be gathered when in their greatest perfection, and the largest and most beautiful of them chosen for the purpose. The following is the method for making red ratafia, fine and soft: Take 12 pounds of the black-heart cherries, 2 pounds black cherries, 1½ pounds raspberries, 1½ pounds strawberries. Pick the fruit from their stalks, and bruise them, in which state let them continue 12 hours; then press out the juice, and to every pint of it add ½ pound of sugar. When the sugar is dissolved, run the whole through the filtering-bag, and add to it 3 pints of proof spirit. Then take 2 ounces of cinnamon, 2 ounces mace, 1 dram cloves. Bruise these spices, put them into an alembic with ½ gallon of proof spirit and 1 quart of water, and draw off a gallon with a brisk fire. Add as much of the spicy spirit to the red ratafia as will render it agreeable; about ¼ is the usual proportion.

◇◇◇

48. RATAFIA DE CAFE

Take ½ pound of roasted coffee, ground, 2 quarts proof spirit, 10 ounces sugar. Digest for a week.

<>

49. RATAFIA DE CASSIS

Take 3 pounds of ripe black currants, ¼ dram cloves, ¼ dram cinnamon, 9 pints proof spirit, 1¾ pounds sugar. Digest for a fortnight.

<>

50. RATAFIA DES CERISES

Take 4 pounds morello cherries, with their kernels bruised, 4 pints proof spirit. Digest for a month, strain with expression, and then add ¾ pound of sugar.

<>

51. RATAFIA DE CHOCOLAT

Take 1 ounce Curaçoa cocoanuts rosted, ½ pound West India cocoanuts, roasted, 1 gallon proof spirit. Digest for a fortnight, strain, and then add 1½ pounds sugar, 30 drops tincture of vanilla.

<>

56 RATAFIA DE THURO D'ORANGE

Take 2 pounds of fresh flowers of orange-tree, 1 gallon proof spirit, 1½ pounds of sugar. Digest for 6 hours.

57. RATAFIA A LA VIOLETTE

Take 2 drams Florentine orris root, 1 ounce archil, 4 pints spirit of wine. Digest, strain, and add 4 pounds sugar.

58. USQUEBAUGH, NO. 1

Usquebaugh is a strong compound liquor, chiefly taken by the dram. It is made in the highest perfection at Drogheda in Ireland. The following are the ingredients: Take 2 quarts of best brandy, ½ pound raisins, stoned, ½ ounce nutmegs, ½ ounce cardamoms, ¼ ounce saffron, rind of ½ Seville orange, ½ pound brown sugar candy. Shake these well every day for at least 14 days, and it will at the expiration of that time be ready to be fined for use.

59. GENERAL DIRECTIONS FOR MAKING CORDIALS

The materials employed in the preparation of cordials are rain or distilled water, white sugar and clean, perfectly flavorless spirit. To these may be added the substances from which the flavor and aroma are extracted, which distinguish and give character to the particular cordial to be made, and also the articles employed as "finings" when artificial clarification is had recourse to. In the preparation or compounding of cordials, one of the first objects which engages the operator's attention is the production of an alcoholic solution of the aromatic principles which are to give them their peculiar aroma and flavor. This is done either by simple infusion or maceration, or by maceration and subsequent distillation, or by flavoring the spirit with essential oils. In the preparation of liqueurs, glycerine has been found to be admirably adapted for preserving the characteristic flavors of those compounds, and it has consequently become the great favorite of this class of manufactures.

◇—◇—◇

60. ANISETTE

To 30 gallons French proof spirit add 4 ounces essence of star anise dissolved in 95 per cent alcohol and 105 gallons syrup of 10° Baume. Stir for ½ an hour, settle and filter.

◇—◇—◇

61. CHAMPION ANISETTE

Put into a barrel 30 gallons 85 per cent alcohol. Add 4 ounces essence of anise seed, which dissolve in 2 gallons 95 per cent. alcohol. Add 103 gallons sugar syrup 10° Baume. Stir 15 minutes and let it rest 4 or 5 days, then filter. Add 2 or 3 sheets of filtering paper.

❖❖❖

62. ANISE SEED CORDIAL

Dissolve 3 drachms of oil of anise seed in 2¾ gallons of 95 per cent alcohol; then add 2½ gallons of fine white syrup, mixed with 4¾ gallons of water. Stir and filter.

❖❖❖

63. CARAWAY CORDIAL

Dissolve 6 drachms oil of caraway in 3 gallons 95 per cent alcohol; add a syrup made of 42 pounds of sugar and 4¾ gallons of water. Filter.

❖❖❖

64. CORDIALS BY DISTILLATION

The solid ingredients should be coarsely pounded or bruised before digestion in the spirit, and this should be done immediately before putting them into the cask or vat; as, after they are bruised, they rapidly lose their aromatic properties by exposure to the air. The practice of drying the ingredients before pounding them, adopted by some workmen for the mere sake of lessening the labor, cannot be too much avoided, as the least exposure to heat tends to lessen their aromatic properties, which are very volatile. The length of time the ingredients should be digested in the spirit should never be less than 3 or 4 days, but a longer period is preferable when distillation is not employed. In either case the time allowed for digestion may be advantageously extended to 10 or 15 days, and frequent agitation should be had recourse to.

——

65. TO MAKE ABSINTHE

Put the following ingredients into a cask:—1½ pounds large absinthe, 2 pounds small absinthe, 2½ pounds long fennel, 2½ pounds star anise (breaking the star only), 2½ pounds green anise seed, 6 ounces coriander seed, and 1 pound hyssop; moisten the whole with a little water, allowing it time to soften and swell; then add 12 gallons 95 per cent alcohol, and steep for 2 or 3 days. Color the product, by steeping in it for 10 or 15 days ½ pound mint leaves, ¼ pound melissa leaves, ½ pound small absinthe, 2 ounces citron peel, and ½ pound bruised liquorice root. Strain and filter.

——

66. FINING WITH ISINGLASS FOR CORDIALS

Take half an ounce of the best isinglass, and dissolve it over a gentle fire, in a pint of water slightly seasoned with good vinegar, or three teaspoonfuls of lemon juice. Beat it from time to time, adding a little of the seasoned water. When you obtain a complete solution, gradually add the foaming liquid to the cordial, stirring all the while. Then stir for 15 minutes after it is all added, and let it rest for 3 days; by that time the cordial will be bright and clear. The above quantity is sufficient to clarify 25 gallons of cordial.

67. TO MAKE SYRUPS FOR THE MANUFACTURE OF CORDIALS & LIQUORS

Take 1 pint of water to every 2 pounds of sugar used; this proportion will make a fine syrup, about 32° Baume, but the manufacturer often requires weaker syrups when preparing inferior cordials, and the easiest method of ascertaining the proper point of concentration is by the use of that variety of Baume's hydrometer, called a saccharometer. Beat up the whites of 2 eggs (if you are clarifying about 10 pounds of sugar, or mix in this proportion) until it is very frothy, and then mix in with the rest.

68. KING'S CORDIAL

Dissolve in ½ pint of proof spirits, 1½ drachms each of the oils of caraway and cinnamon; extract the stones from 3 pounds of black cherries, and mash the fruit in a pan; grate 1 nutmeg; take 2 quarts of Madeira wine, 2 quarts of brandy, and 1 gallon of syrup; mix all together, and color with red saunders wood.

GIN

70. IMITATION SCHIEDAM GIN

Dissolve 3½ drachms oil of juniper in sufficient 95 per cent alcohol to make a clear liquid; add it to 40 gallons French spirits 10 above proof, with 8 ounces orange peel flavoring, 1 quart syrup, and 30 drops oil of sweet fennel.

◇—◇—◇

71. IMITATION OLD TOM LONDON GIN

Dissolve in 1 quart 95 per cent alcohol, 1 drachm oil of coriander, 1 drachm oil of cedar, ½ drachm oil of bitter almonds, ½ drachm oil of angelica, and ½ drachm oil of sweet fennel; add it to 40 gallons French spirit 10 above proof, with 1 pint orange-flower water, 1 quart syrup and 1 drachm oil of juniper dissolved in sufficient 95 per cent alcohol to be clear.

◇—◇—◇

72. TO CLARIFY GIN OR CORDIALS

Pulverize 1 pound ordinary crystals of alum, divide into 12 equal portions, and put up in blue papers marked No. 1. Next take 6 ounces carbonate (the ordinary sesquicarbonate) of soda, divide it into 12 parts and put them up in white papers marked No. 2. In place of the 6 ounces of carbonate of soda, 4 ounces dry salt of tartar may be substituted, but the white papers containing this latter substance must be kept in a dry, well corked bottle or jar. To clarify 30 to 36 gallons gin, dissolve the contents of one of the blue papers, as prepared above in about a pint of hot water, and stir it into the liquor thoroughly. Then dissolve the contents of one of the white papers in about ½ pint hot water, and stir well into the liquor; bung the cask close, and let the whole remain till the next day.

73. TO BLANCH GIN OR OTHER WHITE LIQUOR

By using double the quantity of finings, that is, 2 of each of the powders as laid down in the foregoing receipt, the liquor will be blanched as well as clarified. It is well to recollect, however, that the more finings are employed, the greater the risk of injuring the liquor, which may have a tendency to become flat when "on draught."

74. FININGS FOR GIN

To 100 gallons gin, take 4 ounces roche alum, and put it into 1 pint of pure water; boil it until it is dissolved, then gradually add 4 ounces salts of tartar; when nearly cold, put it into the gin, and stir it well with a staff for 10 minutes. The liquor must not be covered until it is fine; when this is accomplished, cover it up tight to prevent it from losing its strength.

238. PORT WINE

To 10 gallons prepared cider, add 1½ gallons good Port wine, 2½ quarts wild grapes (clusters), 2 ounces bruised rhatany root, ¾ ounce tincture of kino, ¾ pound loaf sugar, ½ gallon spirits. Let this stand 10 days; color if too light, with tincture of rhatany, then rack it off and fine it. This should be repeated until the color is perfect and the liquid clear.

239. RAISIN WINE

5 pounds of raisins, 4 gallons of water. Put them into a cask. Mash for a fortnight, frequently stirring, and leave the lung loose until the active fermentation ceases; then add 1½ pints of brandy. Well mix, and let it stand till fine. The quantity of raisins and brandy may be altered to suit.

240. RAISIN WINE WITH SUGAR

To every gallon of soft water 4 pounds of fresh raisins; put them in a large tub; stir frequently, and keep it covered with a sack or blanket. In about a fortnight the fermentation will begin to subside; this may be known by the raisins remaining still. Then press the fruit and strain the liquor. Have ready a wine cask, perfectly dry and warm, allowing for each gallon one or one and one-half pounds of Lisbon sugar; put this into a cask with the strained liquor. When half full, stir well the sugar and liquor, and put in 1.2 pint of thick yeast; then fill up with the liquor, and continue to do so while the fermentation lasts, which will be a month or more.

⊲◇⊳

241. TO MAKE RASPBERRY WINE

Take your quantity of raspberries and bruise them, put them in an open pot 24 hours; then squeeze out the juice, and to every gallon of the juice put 3 pounds of fine sugar, 2 quarts of canary. Put it into a stein or vessel, and when it has done working stop it close; when it is fine, bottle it. It must stand 2 months before you drink it.

⊲◇⊳

242. RASPBERRY WINE

Pound your fruit and strain it through a cloth; then boil as much water as juice of raspberries, and when it is cold put it to your squeezings. Let it stand together 5 hours, then strain it and mix it with the juice, adding to every gallon of this liquor 2½ pounds of fine sugar. Let it stand in an earthen vessel close covered a week, then put it in a vessel fit for it, and let it stand a month or till it is fine; bottle it off.

265

www.ingramcontent.com/pod-product-compliance
Lightning Source LLC
Chambersburg PA
CBHW032223050726
47591CB00001B/234